GRIM,
GRUESOME
& GRISLY

S. JOHN PESKETT

GRIM, GRUESOME & GRISLY

MURDER AND MAYHEM, CRIME AND CRIMINALS

INCLUDING CELEBRATED CASES OF

M. CLAUDE

CHIEF OF POLICE TO NAPOLEON III

LESLIE FREWIN OF LONDON

First published 1974 by

Leslie Frewin Publishers Limited,
Five Goodwin's Court,
Saint Martin's Lane,
London WC2N 4LL, England

This book is set in Garamond Bold
Photoset, printed and bound in Great Britain by
Weatherby Woolnough Ltd., Sanders Road,
Wellingborough, Northamptonshire

ISBN 0 85632 094 3

CONTENTS

CONTENTS *continued*

INTRODUCTION

'AFTER THE FIRST tribute of sorrow to those who have perished, but at all events after the personal interests have been tranquillised by time, inevitably the scenical features (what aesthetically may be called the comparative *advantages*) of the several murders are reviewed and valued. One murder is compared with another; and the circumstances of superiority – as, for example, in the incidence and effects of surprise, of mystery, etc. – are collated and appraised.'

Thomas De Quincey
'On Murder considered as one of the Fine Arts'

'One single, one return to Sheerdrop Canyon!' says the mild little man accompanied by a forbidding-looking wife, as he pays his money over at the railway ticket office. In an ironmonger's shop a man is ordering a packet of weedkiller, a length of sashcord, a hacksaw, a stout spade and a comfortable garden chair. Two jokes, if my memory serves me, from *The New Yorker*. We realise at once with joyous anticipation that in each case a murder is about to be committed. Do we feel inclined to rush forward and cry 'Stop!' Most certainly not, for there is nothing we enjoy so much as a good murder. We are already following the sequence of events as the nagging spouse is disposed of. Will he get away with it? If not, we still have the spectacle of the murder hunt, the arrest, the trial, the appeal and, until a few years ago, the hangman's drop.

In my youth the English Sabbath was celebrated in millions of homes all over the country, with a midday dinner of roast meats, followed by a cosy afternoon at the fireside reading the Sunday papers which were full of the crimes and trials of the week often illustrated by pencil sketches of the prisoner in the dock. The gorier the murder the greater the enjoyment and this, of course, increased the particular paper's circulation. Long before the advent of the popular Sunday press almost every

7

murder and execution produced a crop of broadsheets, detailing the horrors of the crime and giving an account of the criminal's last hours.

We talk of classic crimes and vintage murders. What makes the crime of Dr Crippen or George Joseph Smith a classic, remembered more than half a century later? The motives in these two cases were entirely different; one was committed for peace of mind and the other for profit. One murderer was a kind little man while the other was a monstrous thug with no thought beyond his bank book. Crippen's case had the drama of the trans-Atlantic flight from justice, thwarted eventually by the first use of wireless telegraphy in a murder hunt. In Smith's we had the triplicated murder plus an element of sex. What better headline than 'The Brides in the Bath'? 'Trunk murders' invariably come into the vintage class. The leather bag oozing blood in the left luggage office at the railway station; the receipt in the murderer's pocket; the severed head in the hatbox; the torso in the Thames, all provide good headline material.

Moreover, as if it were not enough to have the real thing, we have manufactured crimes by the thousand from the *Murders in the Rue Morgue* through Sherlock Holmes and all the other fictional crime hunters to Maigret and the terrors of television, which are nightly brought into our own sitting-rooms in *Z Cars, Softly, Softly, Ironside* and *The Expert*.

Faced with headlines such as 'Councillor urges new housing drive,' 'Kitten saved by local fire brigade' and 'Dismembered corpse found in empty house,' which do we read first? We are all waiting for the 'Hooded Strangler' to strike again, provided of course that he does not select us as his next victims. We look at our watches. The jury has been out three hours. How much longer? What attracts the crowds at Madame Tussaud's? The effigy of General Gordon or Lord Salisbury? Or Christie standing in the squalor of No 10 Rillington Place?

An unsolved crime intrigues us even more. Early in 1914, when I was a small boy, the front-page sensation was the murder of five-year-old Willie Starchfield, whose body was trundled backwards and forwards beneath a carriage seat on the North London Railway between Chalk Farm Station and Broad Street in the City before it was discovered. It is still a minor classic and we shall never know who else was in that carriage or where he got out.

Since August 1914, when the great slaughter of the First World War began, we have witnessed tens of millions of deaths in both world wars. Such statistics are beyond our comprehension; the battlefields, the concentration camps, the air raids, the famines and other natural disasters have merely added noughts to the figures. But the bride in the bath and the little boy in the railway carriage are real. They could have lived in our neighbourhood. By the end of the First World War, France had lost the best of her male population and much of her countryside had been devastated, yet the lunatic manoeuvres of the statesmen at Versailles, ostensibly to prevent a recurrence of the great slaughter, were almost completely ignored in the spectacle of the trial of Henri Désiré Landru which monopolised the headlines. De Quincey was right. We are all connoisseurs when it comes to a good murder.

In this book I have compiled a selection of crimes, many of which took place in France and are generally less well-known than our own Seddons, Haighs or Heaths. I have drawn in places on the *Memoirs of Monsieur Claude,* Chief of Police at the time of Napoleon III, a remarkable character who would have had to be invented by Simenon had he not existed in real life.

Monsieur Claude's highly moral style is very unlike what one would expect from a professional detective, but he usually got his man. Living as he did in the midst of the corruption and skulduggery of the Second Empire, his job inevitably caused him to be involved in politics. At that time few crimes, especially those committed in the higher strata of society, could fail to have political repercussions. Poor Claude always had to go about his business of hunting criminals with one eye on the Imperial Court and the possible effect of scandal on the already crumbling reputation of Napoleon le Petit. In one case he personally removed the embarrassing corpse of the young lover of an influential *grande dame,* a distant relative of the Emperor, from her bed and transferred it to the young man's lodgings, where he could be said to have died as a result of his life of debauchery. This was not far from the truth since he had succumbed from exhaustion, as the virtuous Monsieur Claude reports, 'in the arms of this vigorous matron, this titled Messalina.' However, the outraged reader will be glad to know that the lady in question received her just punishment in due course. She died of an inflammation of the chest which she contracted while visiting the tomb of her deceased lover in the dead of night. Claude is of course the soul of discretion. It is always Madame X or the Marquis de S. He uses initials as profusely as any of the great Russian novelists. His secrecy and preoccupation with the growing unpopularity of his Imperial master were not unjustified. It has been said by more than one historian of the period that the Troppmann case, for instance, helped to topple the Bonaparte dynasty just as the murder of the Duchesse de Praslin was the last of a series of scandals which brought about the flight of Louis-Philippe in 1848.

My murderers range from the bestial Troppmann to the

sentimental but none the less callous La Pommerais (Loving Husband and Murderer). The subjects of some of these studies were not murderers at all. Some are farcical, as in the 'Case of the Photographer's Mistress (La Belle Léonide)' or my own invention 'The Man Who Bought a Tram.' I should add that the story of the tram buyer is not entirely fictitious. It was inspired by a similar swindle which I was told actually happened in Buenos Aires, though my story is set in Brussels.

A number of these cases, both fact and fiction, have already been published in the *London Mystery Magazine* and in the now, alas, defunct *Courier* magazine. I am indebted to my friend, Major Norman Kark of Norman Kark Publications Ltd for his kind permission to reprint them.

CHAPTER ONE

SMOKE IN THE RUE LESUEUR

'Let us meet,
And question this most bloody piece of work,
To know it further.'

Macbeth II (I)

After both great wars this century, a mass-murderer added to the headlines of the world's press a postcript to the greater mass murder which preceded it. While the Treaty of Versailles was being formulated in the Hall of Mirrors, the trial of Landru in the local courtroom kept international issues from the front page in 1919. And in the sorry squabbling and recrimination which followed the liberation of France, Marcel Petiot in 1946 faced the *Cour d'Assises de la Seine,* charged with mass murder on a scale which none but the Gestapo could have equalled.

There was no mystery about Landru. His was a straightforward case of murder for gain, eliminating lonely and loveless middle-aged spinsters and widows for their meagre savings and few sticks of furniture. Petiot, on the other hand, remains a mystery. Was he a squalid murderer for profit, a sadistic fiend with his private death chamber and lime pit, or was he the hero of the Resistance, the stern executioner of the enemies of his country, the Scarlet Pimpernel who operated escape routes out of France under the noses of the Gestapo? Who *were* the victims of the sinister house in the rue Lesueur? Were they some of the sixty-three German officers and enemy agents he claimed to have 'executed' or were they the frightened little people who went there by night, their suitcases packed with valuables, paying large sums for a safe conduct to freedom in South America?

*   *   *

Between two of the stately avenues which converge at the Étoile in the west end of Paris is the rue Lesueur. That is where the story of Dr Marcel Petiot begins. One night early in 1944, when Paris was still under German occupation, neighbours noticed large volumes of smoke of a particularly unpleasant odour coming from the chimney of No 21, a respectable private house. The man who lived next door rang the bell and, receiving no reply, telephoned the police.

The police duly arrived. They were in no great hurry. A chimney on fire was routine stuff. They found the door of No 21 locked. The concierge next door gave them the name and telephone number of the owner, Dr Petiot, rue Caumartin No 66, near the Madeleine. On the door of No 21 the police found a notice to the effect that the owner would be away for a month and that mail should be forwarded to an address in Auxerre. The police still hesitated to break in, so they telephoned the address in the rue Caumartin. It was answered by Madame Petiot, who brought her husband to the telephone. 'Have you broken in yet?' he asked. 'Not yet,' the police replied. 'Well, hold on,' said Dr Petiot, 'I'll be round with the keys at once.'

The police waited in vain for half an hour, and decided to call the fire brigade, who got into the house with the help of a ladder. The gathering crowd waited expectantly until the door was opened from within. Three firemen appeared, their faces white with horror. They had found the first floor deserted, the ground floor crowded with furniture and junk of all kinds, and had then followed the foul smoke to its source in the cellar. The reek of burning flesh guided them to the boilers of the central heating system. One was red hot. Part of a human body protruded from the open door of the furnace. On the floor was another body split down the middle like a carcase in a butcher's shop, and all around were legs, arms, bones, other fragments of human flesh and partly burned skulls.

At that moment a middle-aged little man arrived at the house on a bicycle. It was Petiot, who had been delayed, as it later

15

transpired, burning incriminating papers in the rue Caumartin. He had a good look round, realised that the game was up and made to enter the house. Challenged at the door, he announced that he was the brother of Dr Petiot, the proprietor of the house. The policeman took him in and showed him down to the cellar. He looked steadily at the horrible debris, seeming to note carefully each body or fragment of a body. He looked at an axe, red with blood, hanging near one of the boilers. He seemed quite unmoved. Suddenly he went into action and turned confidentially to one of the policemen.

'Listen, you're a Frenchman, aren't you?' In those days that question had more meaning. Criminals and police had one thing in common; they were Frenchmen in the face of the enemy. The policeman was listening. 'Well, you'd better be careful. These bodies you've just discovered are Germans and collaborators. You've landed yourself in something now. This *would* happen! You've uncovered the execution centre of a Resistance group. The whole lot are underground and will have to be reorganised. Have you told the *Sûreté?*' Yes, the policeman had done so. 'Now, *my* life is in danger,' said Petiot, 'as well as those of a whole crowd of my friends in the Resistance. I'm the head of the group, and have over three hundred traitors' files on my hands. I'll have to go quickly and destroy them.'

The rest of the policemen had gathered round listening to Petiot's dramatic story. What were they to do? Perhaps they should have arrested him. He was at least a valuable witness, and seemed to know so much. But they were Frenchmen. Could they hand over a hero of the Resistance to the Gestapo? One of the policeman then said, 'You'd better beat it quick. We'll sort this out. We haven't seen anyone.' Thus, incredibly, Petiot was enabled to get on his bicycle and disappear. That was the last the police saw of Petiot until after the liberation.

The house at No 21 rue Lesueur then began to give up its secrets. The ground floor was like a secondhand furniture warehouse. The cellar was, as we have seen, a chamber of horrors. But an extension of the main building in the interior yard of the house was even more interesting. There was an office or consulting room behind which a dark passage led to a curious triangular room with no windows. This was the most sinister feature of the whole place. It was a kind of cell with a double door fitted with a chain on the passage side. Each section of the double door was fitted with a lock, but there was no handle on the inside.

On one of the remaining two sides of the cell was another door, also double. The police tried to force it, only to find that it was a false entrance. Behind was a wall and in the wall was a small aperture six feet from the ground, apparently a spy-hole. Set in the wall were eight stout hooks at various heights, which the police decided were for hanging bodies. Beyond the triangular cell were a garage and a lumber-room. The latter was strewn with human remains covered with quicklime. There were bones, hair, teeth and pieces of flesh. Near the garage a pulley fixed in the ceiling carried a rope with an iron chain and hook. This hung over an old cess-pit several feet deep, into which was set a ladder. The pit was half filled with quicklime. Here were more fragments of decomposing human remains.

Someone had to clear up this mess and get every scrap of it to the forensic laboratories. The firemen and policemen could not face it, so a number of gravediggers had to be specially recruited for the job.

At that time the first thought of anyone encountering this

carnage, not to mention the triangular cell with the hooks on the wall, would be, the Gestapo. Their headquarters were only a short distance away in the Avenue Foch. Even the French police thought at first that they had accidently stumbled on a Gestapo interrogation centre. They could hardly imagine that the inoffensive little man who had answered the telephone and obligingly come round on his bicycle could be the instigator of this nightmare. But the Germans had no hand in it.

By the time the police decided to follow the trail of Petiot, he was safely away. The next morning when the police called at No 66 rue Caumartin, Madame Petiot announced that he had not returned since the telephone call of the previous evening. The flat was searched but nothing of value or interest was found beyond a large supply of poisons and five hundred ampoules of morphine. Madame Petiot was released after a futile interrogation and the search moved to Auxerre. Besides the indication in the message on the door in the rue Lesueur, it had been established that a telephone call had been made to Auxerre from the flat in the rue Caumartin on the evening of the discovery. This led them to one Maurice Petiot, the doctor's brother, who was a local radio dealer. No one there had seen Dr Petiot, so the next port of call was to No 18 rue des Lombards, which was the address given for forwarding mail. It proved to be an uninhabited house belonging to Maurice Petiot. Nothing connected with Dr Petiot was found, so the police returned to Maurice Petiot's own abode, which they carefully guarded in case Dr Petiot should turn up. He did not, but early next morning they caught someone else trying to slip in. It was Madame Petiot. Her story was so vague that she was promptly arrested.

It appears that when the police rang the flat in the rue

Caumartin, her husband had told her that human remains had been discovered in the rue Lesueur. He said that he knew nothing about it, packed a bag, sorted out some papers and disappeared. He recommended his wife to do the same. She did not go with him, but seems to have wandered about Paris for a time and finally ended up at Auxerre. She was brought back to Paris with Maurice Petiot. The only information obtained was from Maurice, who confirmed having supplied half a ton of quicklime to his brother, apparently for whitewashing the front of the house. It was evident that they knew very little and were released later.

The next call was on a family called Neuhausen. The husband had been in the habit of sleeping at Maurice Petiot's other house in the rue des Lombards at Auxerre. The police decided to visit the home of the Neuhausens at Courson. There in the attic they found forty-nine suitcases. The concierge at No 23 rue Lesueur later confirmed that he had seen forty-nine suitcases being taken away from No 21 in a small lorry. He was so surprised at the sight that he had counted them. Trust a Paris concierge to know everything that goes on next door! These suitcases were clearly the luggage of the people whose remains had been found at the rue Lesueur. They were removed and the contents examined. There were dozens of men's suits and women's dresses, shirts, socks, fur coats, hats, handkerchiefs, skirts, underclothes, corsets, handbags, gloves and pyjamas.

A catalogue of these personal possessions eventually set the police well on the trail of indentifying the victims. Meanwhile the newspapers had all the headline material they needed for a long time. Despite the hue and cry set up by the press, Petiot was nowhere to be found. It appeared later that he had been living all that time in the centre of Paris.

19

Many doctors were called upon to sort out and, if possible, identify the mass of human remains removed from the rue Lesueur. There were both men and women among the victims. Some had been scalped, and others had had their faces removed with a knife after death to prevent identification. The most interesting thing was that otherwise no trace of violence was found on any of the bodies, no signs of strangulation, of bullets or of any weapon. It was obvious that the bodies had been cut up by someone skilled in anatomy. Eventually, assisted by labels on clothing and information from the families of missing persons, the police were able to compile a list of possible victims.

Born in 1897, Marcel Petiot showed many signs of mental imbalance in his youth. Nevertheless, he was enabled as a discharged invalid from the First World War to study medicine, and qualified as a doctor at the age of twenty-six. His career in medicine took little heed of the Hippocratic oath, though later a number of people were to testify to his skill and devotion. After practice in the country and some dabbling in local politics, he settled in Paris. Here again he was overtaken by lapses into mental instability, and even spent some time in an asylum. He was no ornament to his profession, and it seems incredible now that he managed to avoid being disqualified.

Then came the Second World War and, after the Germans had reached Paris, the persecution of the Jews. Some of these Jews were eventually to find their way to the rue Lesueur. It was a wonderful period for a none-too-scrupulous doctor; drugs and abortions offered a lucrative career. In the early part of the occupation Petiot was twice sentenced, but somehow succeeded in retaining his diploma.

It was in the latter part of 1942 that Petiot saw his opportunity of going into business in a really big way. Many wealthy Jews in Paris at that time knew that their days were numbered. But the good Dr Petiot knew of a secret organisation for getting Jews and others out of the country to a place of safety. Of course it would cost money. The price would be 25,000 francs. Later it went as high as 200,000 francs. All one had to do was to pack one's valuables in a suitcase, sew jewels or banknotes into one's clothes and go secretly at night to No 21 rue Lesueur. Dr Petiot would do the rest. But under no circumstances was the address to be communicated to anyone, not even to one's nearest and dearest. That was the golden security rule. Thus the victims supplied the maximum of loot and carefully covered up their tracks themselves.

The doctor started with a patient of his, a Jewish furrier, but among others he 'helped' were a wealthy banking family and a gangster on the run, together with his mistress. So began the long queue to the rue Lesueur, by way of which all were to reach Buenos Aires and safety. At least, that is what Dr Petiot maintained. Individuals made their way under cover of darkness, their precious belongings in a suitcase, to the doctor's consulting room, through which they passed to the triangular cell? the furnace? the pit of quicklime? or to Buenos Aires and freedom?

Then came the liberation, and who should be fighting at the barricades but Dr Marcel Petiot of the FFI. That at least was definitely established. Later that year he managed to procure by fraud the indentity papers of a Dr Wetterwald, who had been in German captivity and had not been released. Armed with this new name, he joined the army as a lieutenant. About that time an article appeared in a Paris paper about the missing Petiot, accusing him of being a Gestapo agent. Lieutenant

Wetterwald, alias Petiot, wrote an angry reply, which he sent to the offices of the paper. The writing was similar to that found on papers collected at the rue Lesueur and the rue Caumartin. Petiot, who was by now Capitaine Valéry of the Resistance, was discovered when the handwriting of all serving officers in Paris was checked, and he was arrested at last.

Thus, on 18th March, 1946, two years after the discovery at the rue Lesueur, the case of Dr Marcel Petiot opened before the *Cour d'Assises de la Seine.* As at the trial of Landru, a fashionable crowd scrambled for seats at the murder case of the century. Like Landru, Petiot posed for the photographers. It was his big day. Throughout the trial his replies, like Landru's, were witty and accusing, and he was the most self-composed one present.

Petiot had an answer for everything. The triangular cell was merely for his radiotherapy installation. The walls were thick because lead was scarce at the time. Even the bodies were explained away. He found them there when he was released from Fresnes prison after one of his early wartime escapades.

Asked to explain the lime pit, he said he had to get rid of the bodies and fortunately had comrades to help him, but he refused to give the names of any of them. He told the judge that the only reward they would get would be handcuffs for killing a few dozen Germans. Handcuffs for men who deserved the Cross of Liberation! Prosecuting counsel challenged Petiot to bring them into Court and he would guarantee that they got their cross. Petiot refused. He was also unable or unwilling to identify or produce the officer who came from London during the war to train his Resistance group. He stumbled badly over technical details of explosives he was said to have used in his Resistance activities.

The story of his finding the bodies in the house in the rue Lesueur did not go down well and his explanations of his dealings with clients in his escape organisation were less and less convincing, especially when counsel's final question in each case referred to some article or garment found in the cellar or in one of the suitcases. Finally, he admitted 'executing' some of them; 'They were all Gestapo agents and I am proud of having killed them.' But he stuck to his story that the bodies in the rue Lesueur were there when he came out of prison.

The courtroom was like a pawnbroker's shop. The suitcases and all manner of personal property were stacked in evidence. The interminable listing of Petiot's contacts went on. He began to open up a little. Certain Jews fleeing from German persecution were mentioned. They were Germans from Berlin, according to Petiot, and he treated them all alike. They were executed in the Forest of Marly. These Jews had been sent by the Gestapo as *agents provocateurs* to find out about Petiot's Resistance and escape group and he had eliminated them. Others were all right and he helped them to get away. Unfortunately for him some pyjamas belonging to a child from a family said by Petiot to have 'escaped', had been found at the house.

In case after case, the missing were shown to have made their last rendezvous at the rue Lesueur. Over ninety witnesses were called, but none came from Buenos Aires to testify to the efficiency of Dr Petiot's escape route to freedom. No one even sent a postcard. Similarly, there was no confirmation of Dr Petiot's activities in the Resistance. He gave the code-name of his group and referred to other heroic figures of the Resistance. No one had ever heard of them, and no one came forward to say they had been members of the same group. Bitter recriminations filled the court at times. Who were the real heroes of the Resistance and who were those who took the oath to Pétain? Even the judge allowed himself to be drawn into reproaches of this kind.

The horrid picture emerged on one side. The frightened Jews arrived at the doctor's consulting room, the injection given ostensibly for the journey, in reality a fatal drug. The triangular cell at the end of the passage, the lime-pit and the furnace. Through the spy-hole Petiot watched them die. Yet very little money or valuables were found in Petiot's possession. Where did the proceeds go?

On the other side was Petiot, the heroic leader of his Resistance group, executing Gestapo agents and leading the wretched fugitives out of the horror of German-occupied France to the promised land. People who shared a cell with Petiot were called to say that he was almost a saint. The parents of a child he had cared for free of charge over a long period gave evidence of his kindness and generosity. Petiot's advocate showed him as Petiot the hero and patriot. He said he had the right and duty to execute the enemies of his country in time of war.

In vain he repeated Petiot's story that the various Jewish families which had disappeared had come to Paris in very suspicious circumstances. They had stayed at hotels which were known to be Gestapo hideouts. They were Germans and Petiot was justified in protecting his Resistance network. Petiot nodded approvingly as his heroic deeds were enumerated.

The trial dragged on for weeks. Finally, the jury retired. It was late at night, as in the trial of Landru. At last the verdict; Petiot was found guilty.

His appeal was rejected, and soon afterwards the guillotine

awaited him early one morning outside the prison of La Santé. At first it was doubtful how Petiot would be executed, as the guillotine had been damaged in the bombardment of Paris. However, an intact specimen was found somewhere in the provinces and brought to the capital.

It was just before five o'clock in the morning when Petiot was roused from his last sleep He made no confession. 'I am a traveller,' said he, 'taking my baggage with me.' He remained cool to the last. Just before he stepped up to the platform of the guillotine, he turned to those with him and said 'Now, gentlemen, may I give you a last piece of advice? Turn away. This is not going to be a pleasant sight.'

CHAPTER TWO

LA BELLE LEONIDE
THE PHOTOGRAPHER'S MISTRESS
(A TRAGI-COMIC STUDY IN CHEMICAL WARFARE)

TOWARDS THE END OF THE SECOND EMPIRE ABOUT A CENTURY AGO, THERE took place in that picturesque Paris of bombazine and bustles a contest between two women, which once and for all destroys the legend of the fragile Victorian female reaching for her smelling salts and swooning into the embarrassed arms of a reluctant Algernon, Egbert or Clarence. Here is the story. There is a moral in it somewhere, which you must interpret, gentle reader, for yourself.

A prosperous photographer had entertained for some months, as the French official record delicately describes the situation, intimate relations with a young person named Léonide who was giving his wife piano lessons. Monsieur Duhamel, as we shall call him, was young and of an ardent temperament. Léonide, the young piano teacher, was beautiful with a figure which brought tightening of the throat and weakness to the knees of all men who beheld her. And she was alone in the world.

Lessons had scarcely progressed beyond the five finger exercises and a simple rendering of *Au Clair de la Lune* in the key of C before the beautiful young Léonide was listening to the endearments of Monsieur Duhamel. He told her that he was not really married and that he was tired of being bound to a woman by chains which were no more legitimate than his children. He offered her marriage and she, having already been disappointed in love several times, welcomed the prospect of secure married bliss and release from *Au Clair de la Lune* in the key of C.

Alas or *hélas,* if you prefer local colour, the wife of the photographer perceived the intrigue which was developing under her roof, flourished a very genuine marriage certificate under the delicate nose of La Belle Léonide and threw her out.

28

The legal wife had a strong ally in her brother, who apart from his concern for his sister's honour and the future of her children, also had an interest in the photographer's business and was not willing to see it go to pieces for La Belle Léonide. In fact, it was he, and not the vaunted female intuition, who tipped the wife off. We simply must preserve the tradition that it is the wife who finds out last.

So La Belle Léonide departed in floods of tears and stifled reproaches. Soon she found herself at the end of her resources, since she had lost all her other pupils during her dalliance with the licentious photographer. Months went by and at last, after frantic searches, Monsieur Duhamel located her on the point of dying of hunger. He threw himself at her feet. One can almost hear soft music from *La Bohème*. He could not offer her his name now, but he suggested opening forthwith a branch photography studio in Belleville, of which she would be the manageress. She pretended to hesitate, as women do on such occasions, and finally accepted.

Thus she was established as Madame Duhamel at Belleville on the other side of Paris and all went well for a few months. She ran the branch house, the energetic Duhamel ran from one wife to the other, and everyone was happy.

But once again the figure of the brother-in-law, the brother of the genuine Madame Duhamel, was to step in like the Devil in a pantomime. Where should he go to a party one night but to the house of a sculptor friend, at Belleville!

The conversation turned to women and the sculptor said he had a beautiful neighbour, Madame Duhamel, who was the wife of a photographer. In his cups he waxed eloquent, describing curves in the air as sculptors do. 'A magnificent blonde!' he said, 'with the figure of a naiad! Guyon himself must have used her as a model for the seductive bas-reliefs on the Fountain of the Innocents!' The brother-in-law, also in his cups, exclaimed that Madame Duhamel was not blonde but brunette and in any case was the last woman to allow herself to be perpetuated as a naiad, even for Guyon. Then he began to realise what it was all about and plied the now reluctant sculptor for further information. The sculptor admitted that La Belle Léonide – for it was no other – was known to all her customers as Madame Duhamel, even in the presence of the perfidious Duhamel, whom he had seen there in the flesh.

That evening her brother told the whole story to the real Madame Duhamel, who flew into a screaming rage. She demanded the address of La Belle Léonide, seized a bottle of vitriol and departed for Belleville like a regiment of Valkyries. The brother, now belatedly seeing the red light, followed and reached Belleville at the same time as the outraged spouse and her bottle of sulphuric acid.

There, in the combined love-nest and branch of the firm of Duhamel, were La Belle Léonide and the husband, preparing some photographic proofs for the morrow. The horrified couple immobilised by the furious intrusion and their common guilt, stood like two souls on Judgement Day.

Madame Duhamel, the bottle in her hand, made a leap like a lioness on her detested rival. By an instinctive movement, the former piano mistress avoided the first full deadly charge and was only slightly injured. But what is Duhamel doing? You may well ask. About to rush to his mistress's aid, he found himself held fast by our old friend the brother-in-law!

Then the duel began. Léonide, maddened with pain, herself seized a bottle of acid, which was among her professional equipment in the shop, and threw the contents in the face of

Madame Duhamel. That evened things up, you may well say. Then the brother-in-law released for a moment the unhappy Duhamel to go to his sister's aid, but that raving Amazon needed no such assistance. Just as Léonide threw the acid, Madame Duhamel took another flying leap under her guard and wrenched the bottle from the mistress's hand. Throwing her to the floor, she proceeded to tear off the clothing of La Belle Léonide, rending it with her hands and even even using her teeth. When one considers the armoury of clothing women wore in those days, this was no light feat and spoke well for the energy and the dentation of the raving Madame Duhamel.

Having practically undressed the screaming Léonide, she held her on the floor and began industriously to anoint her all over the body with the remaining contents of the bottle. The more the helpless victim screamed, the more the redoubtable Madame Duhamel poured it on.

But what in the name of Heaven is Duhamel doing? You may well ask again. It's the brother-in-law once more, who held him fast and against whom he struggled in vain, crying out with pity, anguish and remorse and overcome with horror.

Finally, the screams and cries of the wretched Léonide attracted attention just as the now almost lunatic Madame Duhamel was trying to open the eyes of the girl to pour in the last drops of vitriol and blind her. As the neighbours broke in, La Belle Léonide gave no sign of life and one can be quite sure that she no longer resembled the naiad of the sculptor's dreams.

The Paris police, complete with *juge d'instruction,* arrived. The victim was removed, more dead than alive, and the rest of the company was taken into custody.

When, after a long illness, the unfortunate Léonide recovered sufficiently to speak, the trial took place. It was dominated by the unconquerable Madame Duhamel. Léonide refused to say anything against the now rather less ardent Duhamel, who blamed the brother-in-law. At the Tribunal, things looked black for him, but it was Madame Duhamel, who by her vehemence and masterful control of the whole scene caused him to be declared *hors de cause*. 'May the heavens break to reveal the truth, since the broken heart of a mother cannot persuade you!' she roared at the judges.

In the end, the case was settled by the defendants Duhamel and his wife being condemned to support the injured Léonide. So Léonide had a guaranteed pension from the Duhamel coffers. Public opinion was divided between Léonide the martyr and Madame Duhamel the heroine. Both women had a fair share of the centre of the stage at the end, while the former dashing hero Duhamel, cowering in the wings, had to put his hand in his pocket thereafter to support the no longer *belle* Léonide and pay for his wife's revenge. What was worse, he had to go on living with his wife, probably the greatest punishment for any of the actors in this eventful history. Thus we make our own little Hell.

This is a true story from the archives of the Paris police and at the very least is one more good argument against chemical warfare.

CHAPTER THREE

TWO CHICKENS
AND
ONE RED
HERRING

AFTER A BATH OF BLOOD AND ACID LET US TURN FOR A BRIEF INTERVAL
of light relief in Italian comedy.

The Supreme Criminal Court in Naples was in session. It was
mid-morning and it looked as if the case would go on till about
two o'clock. It was a hot day and the President was having an
argument with three of the advocates at once. The prisoner,
who was charged with robbery with violence, stood
philosophically in the dock, heavily guarded. At the back of the
court in the public seats sat half the criminal population of
Naples, including most of the accused man's numerous family.
The latter were not at all pleased with Gennaro for being
caught and far from satisfied with the way the case was going.
The President was in bad humour that morning. He glanced
impatiently at the clock. It had stopped. 'Will someone tell me
the time?' he roared. 'I left my watch at home this morning!'
One of the advocates told him it was half past ten and the case
continued.

Shortly afterwards, one of the least reputable of Gennaro's
male relatives was seen to leave the court. Twenty minutes later,
he presented himself at the house of the President. He was
carrying a parcel. He asked to see the Signora and was at once
shown into the drawing room of the President's wife. 'Signora,
I have been sent from the court. The President presents his
compliments and asks me to bring you these two chickens. The
President has two unexpected visitors, whom he is bringing
home to lunch soon after one o'clock. He asks you to be good
enough to have these two chickens cooked ready for lunch.
And the President says may he please have his watch, which he
left at home this morning?'

The Signora took the chickens and sent Maria Modesta to get
the President's watch, which he had left in his bedroom. The

man took it and placed it carefully in his pocket. He noticed that it was of solid gold and worth a fair sum of money. The Signora thanked him and he made off.

That might well be the end of the story, but two hours later he was back again. He asked to see the Signora once more and was shown in. He again brought the compliments of the President and thanks for the watch. The President now wished to say that, as it was such a fine day, he had decided to take his friends into the country for a picnic and he would like to have the two cooked chickens, wrapped in grease-proof paper.

The Signora bustled off, made a neat package of the two cooked chickens and gave them to the man, who departed and was never seen again. Nor were the chickens. Nor was the watch.

The lesson of this is that in conjuring or in business it is sound psychology to employ a red herring to cause a distraction from the main purpose of the operation. Moreover, it is the ideal in business to get back your investment together with the profit.

The sad part of this story, as a comment on human nature, is that it is true. It was told to me by one of the advocates with whom the President was arguing that morning.

CHAPTER FOUR

LA POMMERAIS:

LOVING HUSBAND AND MURDERER

AN EVER-RECURRING MYSTERY IN THE ANNALS OF CRIME IS THE GENTLE murderer, the deadly killer who is at the same time the kindest of husbands and the adored father of a family. It is curious that many such murderers have been doctors. The classic split personality of fiction was a doctor, Henry Jekyll. Dr Ruxton was devoted to his children. Dr Crippen was a kindly character who successfully protected his co-defendant. Dr Petiot, whom we have already met, was spoken of as a ministering angel by some of the witnesses at his trial. The notorious Dr Pritchard was a pious and tearful fellow, who quoted the Bible freely and, be it said, mainly for his own justification.

Yet it must be admitted that the crime of murder is all the more heinous when perpetrated by one who has taken the Hippocratic oath.

An outstanding example was the poisoner, Dr Edmond de la Pommerais, who was run to earth by the redoubtable Monsieur Claude. The exploits of Maigret are small beer compared with the adventures and encounters which Monsieur Claude packed into a dozen volumes of memoirs. In this chronicle of his long career appear some of the most disreputable names in the history of evil-doing. La Pommerais ranks high in this sinister directory.

He was a fraud from the beginning. His real name was Lapommerais but, by a self-ennoblement while still a student, he became de la Pommerais and even procured a bogus parchment to support his claim to blue blood. Later he was to promote himself to Count. The son of a modest country doctor from the Loiret, he duly passed his examinations and established himself in Paris. It was a very humble practice. With the expensive tastes which accompanied his social ambitions, he soon ran into debt. In fact his situation would have been even more disastrous had it not been for the help he received from one of his mistresses, Madame de Pauw, who had a small income of her own.

Medicine at a few francs a visit proved a most unrewarding occupation and La Pommerais soon turned to other activities. An attempt to make money out of a gaming establishment at Monaco failed. He next got himself nominated as doctor attached to the benevolent society of the parish of St Thomas Aquinas. Having been caught with his hand in the cash box of the society, he somehow managed to get out of this first venture into crime. He paid back the money to the parish authorities but, as this worthy action coincided with the death of another of his mistresses, apparently from typhoid while in his care, it might have been more than a coincidence.

It was the Monaco business which first brought La Pommerais officially to the notice of Monsieur Claude, though the two men had met by a strange accident some years before. Monsieur Claude was on this occasion in a fiacre with a mysterious Madame X. Always the anonymous initial! I may add that this journey was strictly in connection with his official duties. Their fiacre collided with another vehicle going in the opposite direction. The two cabbies entered into the usual Parisian exchange of injurious epithets. Monsieur Claude looked out of the window to see that in the other cab were obviously – that is obviously to Monsieur Claude – two guilty lovers, a young man and a woman who appeared anxious to conceal her identity. Monsieur Claude had occasion to reprove his own cabby, who announced himself as one Collignon, a model of probity, when the Chief of Police threatened to have him arrested if he did not at once cease his rioting and disengage the wheels of his own cab from the wheels of the other.

As the other cab was about to move on, the young man handed his perfumed card, decorated with a coat of arms, to Monsieur Claude with a word of thanks. The card bore the name of Dr Edmond de la Pommerais. Six months later, Monsieur Claude was to sit at the assizes at the trial of the brutal murderer, Collignon the cabby! Nine years later, he was to lead Edmond de la Pommerais to the guillotine. Such dramatic encounters were all in a day's work for Monsieur Claude.

The affair of the *Société des Bains de Monaco* was a fraudulent share deal in which La Pommerais was involved with a certain Prato, who had ennobled himself to be the Marquis d'Arnezano. In fact the self-ennobled Count was taken in by the self-ennobled Marquis. Suffice it to say that a number of well-placed people were also mixed up in the unsavoury business and, fortunately for La Pommerais, it was hushed up.

It meant however that La Pommerais was still hard up. Thus in 1861 he married a Mlle Dubizy, who brought him a dowry of a hundred and fifty thousand francs. This was badly needed to pay off creditors and to keep his mistress, Madame de Pauw, whose own resources were limited. However, the newly wed Madame de la Pommerais adored her brilliant and handsome husband. Her happiness was at first shared by her mother, who found her son-in-law the most charming of men, but her delight in the happy marriage of her daughter was short-lived. Two months after the marriage Madame Dubizy died after a brief illness, diagnosed as cholera by her devoted son-in-law. His grief was softened by the inheritance of a million and a half francs.

Our hero was now rich beyond his dreams, so rich that it went to his head. For a time he frequented the highest ranks of what passed for Society in the Second Empire. He maintained a number of mistresses, among them the wife of the Marquis d'Arnezano, who was the lady in the fiacre some years back! Unfortunately he saw himself as a great financier and in eighteen months the whole fortune had disappeared in stock exchange speculations. He was worse off than before.

Madame de Pauw had become the mistress of La Pommerais after the death of her husband who had been attended by La Pommerais in his professional capacity. After his acquisition of Madame Dubizy's wealth, La Pommerais decided on a most ingenious scheme not only to enrich himself further but to rid himself of Madame de Pauw. This involved playing on her simple, trusting nature and her love for her three young children. He proposed that she should take out an insurance of five hundred and fifty thousand francs payable on her death. She would then feign a serious illness, which would alarm the underwriters. They would then agree to the cancellation of the policy in exchange for an annuity, which she and La Pommerais would share. La Pommerais put up the money for the first premium.

So the trusting Madame de Pauw put on her act of a serious illness brought on by an imaginary fall. She thought that she would have to stay in bed for a week and her children's future was assured. The doctors who examined her spoke of internal lesions. La Pommerais expressed his professional view that she was dying. However, far from negotiating or allowing Madame de Pauw to negotiate with the insurance company, La Pommerais kept her secluded for six weeks, during which time he poisoned her. She died, to quote the dramatic Monsieur Claude, after a last night spent with the infamous doctor, who had given her the kiss of death!

It is hardly necessary to add that Madame de Pauw's modest fortune plus the insurance had been bequeathed to La Pommerais. But this time he had gone too far. The insurance company became suspicious and opened an enquiry. Digitalin was found in the mortal remains of Madame de Pauw. The body of Madame Dubizy was then exhumed and more traces of digitalin were discovered. La Pommerais was arrested and charged with murder.

* * *

Since the affair of the *Société des Bains de Monaco*, Monsieur Claude had maintained contact with La Pommerais, mainly to keep an eye on him, and had even been on visiting terms. In fact La Pommerais had solicited Claude's support for the purpose of obtaining an appointment as prison medical officer. Through all this rake's progress, his young wife had remained devoted to what she imagined to be the ideal husband. So Claude found himself in the unenviable position of having to go to the home of La Pommerais and arrest him there in the presence of his wife. As a guest of long standing he could not bring himself to do this. He thought up a stratagem, which would deceive the wife and possibly La Pommerais himself; he used as a pretext the proposed prison appointment. He called on La Pommerais and in the course of conversation suggested that they should go together to see the Governor of the Mazas prison, as the latter had been raising some difficulty. The wife was puzzled but more or less deceived. La Pommerais knew that the game was up. He followed Claude, who showed him the warrant once they were in the cab together. La Pommerais swore that he was innocent, reproached Claude for the wrong he had done his wife and said he ought to have shot him for it. He was the loving husband and she the devoted wife to the end. Yet he could be so unfeeling that, when it was mentioned later that he had taken the precaution of removing his portrait from the table beside the deathbed of his mistress, he explained the action by saying, 'It was a pretty frame. I wanted to put a picture of my child in it before giving it to my wife.'

After La Pommerais had been sentenced to death, his wife made every effort to save him, even to the extent of appealing to the Empress Eugénie. It is said, though it does not appear in the memoirs of Monsieur Claude, that the Emperor did promise a remission of the death sentence. The glad news was conveyed to La Pommerais in the condemned cell. But Napoleon III, weak as ever, was forced to go back on his word when he met the accusing faces of the *Commission des Grâces.* Thus the murderer who had killed twice was condemned twice.

Yet he loved his wife and she loved him despite everything. As he was being prepared for the end, the Abbé Crozes read him a long and loving letter from his wife. Before he mounted the scaffold, La Pommerais had a lock of his hair cut off. He left it for his wife after pressing it to his lips. As he died, he spoke her name, the name he had whispered to the priest as he embraced him before being thrust onto the plank of the guillotine, Clotilde!

Man finds the world full of mysteries but surely the greatest mystery is Man.

CHAPTER FIVE

THE GHOSTS OF GAMBAIS

EARLY ONE MORNING IN FEBRUARY 1922, WHEN THE REVEILLE WAS sounding in a nearby barracks, a little, bald-headed man with a dramatic-looking beard was dragged out into the yard of the prison of St Pierre at Versailles, quickly lifted onto the guillotine and decapitated. Despite all police precautions to keep unauthorised spectators away, just at that moment a tram rumbled past the prison. It was filled with workmen, who were thus given an unexpected grandstand view of the judicial death of Henri Désiré Landru.

In addition to the workmen and the official observers, the ghosts of at least ten women may well have been present. There were probably more than that but the official indictment lists only ten women and one boy, for the murder of whom Landru was condemned.

Fifty years have gone by since those women and the boy, who was the son of one of them, disappeared. Though their personal belongings were found in Landru's possession, no trace of their bodies was ever discovered and to this day not one of them has reappeared. The only man who knew how they died and where their mortal remains lie carried his secret with him when he took his single ticket to an unknown destination that February morning. In life Landru always took a return ticket for himself and a single for his victim. Again and again in the notebook of this methodical little mass-murderer occurs the entry: one single/one return Gambais. He knew they would never come back from that villa near Paris.

It is said that at his trial, his counsel, whose main defence was that no bodies had been found, pointed dramatically at a door of the courtroom to suggest that at any moment the missing women could appear there. All eyes turned expectantly to the door, save Landru's. He alone knew for certain that

Thérèse Laborde-Line, Anna Collomb. Célestine Buisson, Marie Marchadier and the rest of that sorry company of lonely women would never walk through that door.

Landru's story is a long one. It has often been told but never loses its fascination for the connoisseur. It took nearly three years to assemble the evidence covering the eleven victims on his charge sheet; three years of unravelling the almost incredible tangle of negotiations with about three hundred women. Innumerable relatives had to be hunted out, piles of pitiful relics indentified. Furniture, false hair, jewellery, ration cards, post office bank books and clothing were collected until the courtroom took on the appearance of the Paris Flea Market. Interminable interrogations of Landru himself yielded nothing. When pressed, he invariably retreated behind the excuse that a gentleman never tells of his gallant exploits or betrays a confidence. His notebook, he said, was a record of business transactions with widows and others who had furniture to dispose of. His marriage bureau activities, he freely admitted, were merely a ruse to contact suitable clients for his secondhand trade.

Landru graduated from petty swindling to wholesale murder. Somehow he managed to avoid military service during the First World War. With far more killing going on not so far from Paris, he had ample opportunity to pursue his own private killings undetected. In a city like Paris in wartime there were many displaced and missing people. There was no time to trace obscure widows who disappeared while the war casualty lists grew day by day and when everyone's efforts were directed towards getting enough food and clothing.

His method was to advertise in matrimonial columns. He had a stock of standard letters for the gullible widows who thought they had found romance and security at last. He maintained a series of post boxes and varied his names and addresses throughout the war. Sometimes he would meet the victim, extract what money he could and abandon her on a street corner on some flimsy excuse; or he would find her unsuitable or perhaps too suspicious and call off the deal. Those were the fortunate ones. Others who had a small income or a savings bank book or who possessed a few sticks of furniture were taken off to his villa, either at Vernouillet or later at Gambais. And it was always one single and one return.

How many women were disposed of in this way will very probably never be known. Finally the war came to an end and with it the conditions most favourable to Landru's 'business'. Even so, he carried on and might have continued his career for years but for a chance encounter. The sister of one of the missing women happened to see him in a china shop in the rue de Rivoli. She had met him when her sister, Célestine Buisson, had announced her romance with the mysterious business-man. She had even accompanied her on a visit to Gambais. She went to the police.

The bearded customer in the china shop had given an address in the rue Rochechouart, where he was living with a young woman called Fernande Segret, who was apparently not destined for the fatal visit to Gambais. With that address *l'Affaire* Landru began. It not only made criminal history; it relegated the Treaty of Versailles to the back pages of the newspapers. Now that the great killing was over, society was able to give its attention and judgement to the individual efforts of Henri Désiré Landru.

The almost farcical trial and the near riots in and outside the courtroom as the proceedings slowly progressed to the dramatic death sentence were very little credit to a civilised country. But the nightmare of wartime was over and France turned its attention gleefully to the Grand Guignol tragi-comedy which Landru had written for them.

How could this small scrap of a man swindle, rob and murder on such a scale while living a family life as a devoted husband and father of four children? Until he installed Fernande Segret as his mistress in the flat in the rue Rochechouart, all the proceeds of his crimes were faithfully handed to his wife Marie-Catherine, like the pay packet of any workman; and there was always pocket-money for the children. It is clear that for all of them he had the greatest affection. Yet the timetables in his notebook, which he kept methodically and in which he recorded the last centime, show that he was able to leave his family on some pretext or other, handle the current matrimonial deal with the subsequent realisation of the sale of the furniture or the withdrawal of the victim's savings, dispose of a body and be back again in the family circle in a day or two, as if he had merely slipped out to do some shopping. In addition to this, the notebook gives crowded lists of rendez-vous, often at short intervals, which involved scurrying all over Paris, to meet prospective clients who had replied to his advertisements. He carried on an enormous correspondence based on his stock of standard love letters. Yet with all this activity he made little more than a bare living. His family were continually moving from one wretched habitation to another and always he had to scrape around to provide housekeeping money and pay the rent. Apart from the balance-sheet aspect of Landru's career, one can only feel amazement not only at the lack of moral scruple but at the sheer physical stamina of this sinister little ferret.

The final mystery was the disposal of the bodies. A year after Landru's execution, a strange auction of the débris left by Landru was held at Versailles. Among the miscellaneous articles sold to souvenir-hunters was a small rusty stove. It finally went for four thousand two hundred francs, though it would have fetched scarcely a hundred in the Flea Market. It was said that it had been acquired by the Muśee Grévin, which is the Paris equivalent of Madame Tussaud's.

It was of course assumed that the stove had been used to burn the bodies. At the villas at Vernouillet and Gambais, there had been complaints during Landru's tenancies of smoking chimneys which caused unpleasant smells in the neighbourhood, but no official investigation was made at the time.

Now it has been shown in countless murder cases how extremely difficult, it not impossible, it is to destroy a human body completely. The alternative is to hide it in a place where it is never likely to be found. The few scraps of bones found at Gambais were inconclusive. Landru had therefore found some means of leaving no trace whatever. For his small build, Landru was a man of great energy, as we have seen. Nevertheless he could hardly have been able to transport eleven or more bodies elsewhere, nor could he have found a secure hiding-place so close to Paris. It can only be assumed that he worked through days and nights dismembering, burning in small quantities and then distributing the ashes far afield on his strange wanderings. It would fit in with the workings of his meticulous, little notebook-mind. At one time he possessed an old car, which could have helped him in this task.

How Landru murdered his victims will never be known. These women had sufficient faith in him to accompany him to a lonely villa in the country. They were full of their romantic dreams of bliss and security with their new-found lover or husband. The rest must have been easy. Survivors who had not made the journey to Vernouillet or Gambais spoke of Landru's charm of manner, his amusing ways, his loving attentions, his parlour tricks, his love of opera and even his pleasant singing voice. Those who came to learn how easily the lamb could turn into a ravening wolf did not survive to tell how he did it.

It is conceivable that somewhere on the other side of the Styx the shade of Henri Désiré Landru may meet the ghosts of Gambais. It will prove far more uncomfortable for him than the quick flash of the knife in the prison yard at Versailles in 1922.

CHAPTER SIX

MURDER OR SUICIDE:
THE CALAS CASE

On 10th march 1762, in the place saint-georges at toulouse a man was broken on the wheel. In the whole history of man's inhumanity to man, there is perhaps nothing quite so savage as judicially breaking a man on the wheel. The criminal is tied, face upwards, to a horizontal wheel or St Andrew's cross and his bones are broken by the executioner with an iron bar. It is not necessary to go into further details. It is a shocking thing to realise that this happened as recently as the lifetime of my grandfather's grandfather. It is still more shocking to know that the man who was executed in this brutal way in Toulouse in 1762 was probably innocent. That man was Jean Calas and his story has gone down in history as the Calas case.

It was a period of religious intolerance in that part of France. Although the Massacre of St Bartholomew had taken place nearly two hundred years before, the spirit of St Bartholomew's Eve was by no means dead. Catholics in the capital of Languedoc were still anti-Protestant, and Jean Calas was a Protestant.

The story begins in the house of Jean Calas, who was a successful draper, in the rue des Filettiers. There he lived with his large family in relative comfort. He had four sons and two daughters. His business was conducted on the ground floor and he lived in the upper part of the house.

One evening in October 1761, the Calas parents and two of their sons had been sitting at table since seven o'clock together with a friend of the Calas sons, David Lavaysse. About eight o'clock, one of the sons, Marc-Antoine, left the room presumably to go to a café in accordance with his usual custom. Talk continued at table for about an hour, when Pierre Calas got up to conduct David Lavaysse to the door. When they arrived downstairs they found to their horror that Marc-An-

54

toine, instead of going to the café, had carefully folded his coat and waistcoat and hanged himself at the entrance to the shop. They cut him down and gave the alarm. Jean Calas came running down the stairs with his wife and an old serving woman to find the body of their son lying there. They tried to revive him and threw water in his face, but Marc-Antoine was beyond recall. Pierre rushed off to find a doctor, who arrived and pronounced Marc-Antoine to be dead. He examined him and found no obvious cause of death until he perceived under the man's black cravat the marks of a ligature. 'Your son has been hanged or strangled!' he announced to the agonised parents. 'But who could have done it? The bolts are on the outside door' Jean Calas replied. 'Who could have done it?'

The servant's cries had roused the neighbourhood and the neighbours were by no means friendly towards the Protestant Calas, who was known to have argued with one of his sons over religious matters. Five years earlier, his son, Louis, had left the paternal roof to become a Catholic. This was said to have caused violent family quarrels. The father had refused to maintain his son and a law case had eventually been brought against the father, as a result of which, in September 1761, Jean Calas had finally agreed to pay his son an annual pension. It was also known that Marc-Antoine was subject to fits of melancholy. The story spread almost from the beginning of the enquiry that Jean Calas, thinking that Marc-Antoine was about to join his brother Louis in the Catholic faith, had murdered him in a dispute.

The enquiry was conducted by one David Beaudrigue. He established that on the fatal evening there were six people in the house; Jean Calas and his wife, the sons Marc-Antoine and Pierre, the guest and an old servant. The two daughters were away with friends in the country. Donat, another son, was an apprentice at Nîmes, and, as we already know, Louis had left home.

David Beaudrigue was a kind of examining magistrate. According to the unanimous evidence given to him by the occupants of the house, the outer door was bolted and it was clear that no one could get in unobserved. All those present confirmed the finding of the body and the fact that the coat and waistcoat had been removed. Rather curiously they appeared to wish to avoid the disgrace of a suicide in the house and at first gave the impression that the body had been found lying where it was when the doctor arrived. This may well be considered a curious circumstance. Although it is understandable that people in general do not like admitting to a suicide in the family, it does seem strange that here were six people concerting in misleading evidence right from the start. However, the examining magistrate waited for the doctor's report, which stated definitely that Marc-Antoine Calas had died from hanging.

Then the whole of the family present went back on their former statements and said they had departed from the strict truth only because they were anxious that the body should not be buried ignominiously, as suicides were. They said that Marc-Antoine was a failure in life, that he was given to fits of melancholy and thought only of death which he had finally sought by his own hand. They admitted then that he had been found hanging. It was not a good beginning.

David Beaudrigue was far from satisfied. He caused the whole scene of the tragedy to be carefully examined. It appeared that no chair or stool had been found nearby, where the dead man might have kicked it away. The witnesses asserted that Marc-Antoine's feet were almost touching the ground when he was discovered. Another strange thing was that the room where the suicide took place was in complete darkness. Beaudrigue examined the door, from a peg on which the body was said to have hung. He maintained that it could not possibly have held the weight of a man writhing in the throes of strangulation. In addition, he noted that, where the peg was fixed to the door, the dust had been undisturbed over a long period.

It must be admitted that Beaudrigue had some grounds for suspicion. The witnesses had lied at first and had then refuted their original statements. They had been unanimous in saying that Marc-Antoine had been found lying in the passage and that his clothes were carefully folded close by. Then they said that he was found hanging. Beaudrigue could not believe that a man would carefully fold up his clothes in a pitch dark room and, above all, that he would put on a black cravat, when it was well known that Marc-Antoine never wore a black cravat! After all, a man about to hang himself is not likely to put on any kind of cravat. 'Did you cut him down?' asked Beaudrigue. They could not remember. 'Then why was the rope intact?' insisted Beaudrigue. He was far from satisfied.

Despite Calas's protestations of innocence, the inquiry went forward. Witnesses who might be able to shed some light on the affair were summoned under pain of excommunication. So the usual gossips appeared. One had heard the cry 'Assassin, Assassin!' Another had heard someone shout, 'They're strangling me!' Two women claimed to have seen Jean Calas holding his son by the neck that day and saying 'You rascal, this will cost you your life!' Even the mother was accused of saying, at the time of Louis's departure, 'If I had known, I would have strangled him!' But Jean Calas denied everything and stated categorically, 'Marc-Antoine had no intention of becoming a Catholic.' More gossips turned up to say that they had seen Marc-Antoine at Mass and showing other signs of partiality for the Catholic faith. Jean replied that they had mistaken Louis for Marc-Antoine. Then other witnesses came forward to deny the evidence of the first gossips and to support the statements of Jean Calas. Nevertheless, Jean Calas, his wife and the son Pierre were condemned to the *question ordinaire et extraordinaire* which simply meant examination by torture. They appealed successfully against this. However, despite further evidence in his favour, Calas was eventually brought to trial for the murder of his son.

In that atmosphere of religious prejudice, witnesses for the defence were either suppressed or afraid to testify. Finally, at the trial in February 1762, Jean Calas was found guilty. The Parlement of Toulouse sentenced him to be broken on the wheel. Right to the last moment Beaudrigue hoped to extract a confession from Calas and was even present when he was later tortured. He implored him to confess and name his accomplices. 'I am innocent!' declared Calas, 'and could not have had any accomplices.' Beaudrigue went so far as to accompany him to the place of execution, which seems to indicate that he had doubts and hoped to have them cleared up at the last minute. Even the priest failed to obtain a confession. 'Do you think, Father, that I would kill my own son?' Calas asked him.

So Jean Calas was taken in a cart to the Place Saint-Georges. The same morning he had been dragged, dressed in a shirt only and barefooted, with a rope round his neck, to hear the condemnation in the Judgment Hall. There he was tortured but did not falter in his protestations of innocence.

At the Place Saint-Georges he was tied to a St Andrew's cross. Afterwards his broken body was to be placed on a wheel until he was dead. As the executioner went about his horrid task, Calas cried out for pardon for his accusers, who had been deceived, and called on God to receive his soul. Even the executioner was touched and paused, asking him to confess and promising him a quick death. But Calas continued to deny his guilt. Before he died, he said that Our Lord had died a worse death and He was innocent too. So why should Jean Calas complain?

The judges of Toulouse were still not satisfied. They had deferred sentence on the other accused members of the Calas family in the hope that Jean Calas would denounce them by admitting his own guilt. Pierre was condemned to banishment; the two daughters were placed in convents; and the property of Jean Calas was confiscated. The youngest son, Donat, escaped to Geneva and there enlisted the interest and sympathy of Voltaire. Though subsequent evidence from reliable sources was produced in favour of Jean Calas, it was Voltaire who finally, three years later, obtained from Paris a reversal of the judgment against Jean Calas. The Parlement of Paris quashed the judgment of the Parlement of Toulouse. Voltaire's intervention in this affair is quite a story in itself. One presumes that he really believed that Marc-Antoine Calas committed suicide. Or did he take up the cudgels for the sheer joy of being in a fight, like the Irishman in the story?

Suffice it to say that the innocence of Jean Calas was established officially. Louis XV followed the case for his rehabilitation with the greatest interest and gave generous compensation to the widow, the sons, daughters and the old servant.

So all ends happily, except of course for Jean Calas. Yet lingering doubts remain. How did Marc-Antoine die? Was he murdered by Pierre Calas and David Lavaysse, who were supposed to have found him hanging? Was Jean Calas 'covering up' to save his son and David? Or did Marc-Antoine somehow contrive to hang himself in a fit of melancholy? We shall never know. Of the two verdicts, one stating that Jean Calas was guilty and the other proclaiming his innocence, we must be the judges. If Jean Calas was innocent, we must take him out of our category of convicted murderers and substitute his judges in our rogues' gallery. For the real villains were not always those standing in the dock. The nightmare waxwork figures in their ecclesiastical or judicial gowns, who stood by the rack and ordered another turn of the screw or had one more wedge hammered in between the prisoner's bound ankles; those who held up a crucifix to the man burning at the stake and called on him to confess and name his accomplices so that more could burn; these incredibly were the contemporaries of Pascal, of Newton, of Voltaire, of Descartes and so many others who were then thinking centuries ahead and whose philosophies were temporarily drowned in the shrieking of exorcists casting out imaginary devils.

I suppose we can derive some satisfaction from the fact that the zealous Beaudrigue fell into disgrace after the reversal of the judgment. This caused him to lose his reason and he died, as Marc-Antoine Calas probably died, by his own hand.

CHAPTER SEVEN

THE TROPPMANN HORROR

ON 25TH NOVEMBER, 1869, NEAR THE RUINS OF THE CASTLE OF HERRENFLUCH in Alsace, a group of men, which included two magistrates from Belfort, the Imperial Prosecutor Munschina, the examining magistrate Bardy, the Commissioner of Police from Cernay, Souvras, the secretary of Monsieur Claude (chief of the Paris *Sûreté*), aided by twenty local workers, had been looking for a body.

Towards evening, a cry from one of the searchers brought them all hurrying to a spot almost hidden by bushes and undergrowth. No doubt on the evidence of his secretary, Monsieur Claude dramatically describes a flight of crows which betrayed the grave of a murdered man. Does it not say in St Luke that 'wheresoever the body is, thither will the eagles be gathered together'? These funereal creatures, as Monsieur Claude describes them, seemed reluctant to abandon their feast. The leader of the searchers leapt forward, as the last crow flew off, to discover some fragments of cloth, a brass button and the toes of a man's boots. It was by then too late to dig the body out, so guards were posted and the delicate task of exhumation was left to the following day.

On the morrow the party returned, accompanied by two doctors, and the gruesome work began. At first, all that could be distinguished was a mass of black clothing; then the man's livid face. He was lying on his back in sodden reddish earth which was infested with innumerable worms. The body was bent so that the legs almost touched the head. As the legs were moved there was seen to be crouched on the chest of the corpse an enormous toad, which one of the doctors seized and threw high into the air. What a loss to the Gothic novel when Monsieur Claude joined the police! The ruined castle, the sinister flight of crows in the evening light, the putrescent body, the worms and finally the toad; all this is pure Horace

Walpole and Ann Radcliffe. Was the presence of this unclean beast, asks Monsieur Claude, the symbolic revelation of the impurity which, before this horrible *dénouement,* was said to have cemented the spontaneous, intimate and mysterious association of these two men? He is speaking of the murderer, whom he has under lock and key in Paris, and the man now lying in the wet earth of Alsace. However, for all Monsieur Claude's rhetorical style, this was no laughing matter. The discovery of this man's body was the culminating piece of evidence in one of the most frightful crimes ever recorded.

The face of the dead man presented a terrifying picture of decomposition. One eye had disappeared and maggots crawled in the orbit. The other was still there under the eyelid. The nose was flattened and the moustache came away at a touch. The mouth was filled with earth. There were no wounds, no blood and no marks of violence.

These were the remains of one Jean Kinck, father of six children who, with their mother, had been found murdered not long before on the outskirts of Paris. This was thus the eighth body to be found, and the eighth victim of one of the most sensational murders in the history of crime.

For France the year 1869 was momentous. The grotesque Emperor Napoleon III had almost run his course and France stood before the defeat and humiliation of Sedan, from which she has not recovered to this day. A mounting series of crimes and scandals had undermined all confidence in the Emperor and his government. Of these the murder of the entire Kinck family, a tragedy of incomparable horror, was to be one more blow to a tottering administration. It appeared at that time as an omen of the wrath to come, which did indeed come in the general disintegration after 1870.

When the abolition of capital punishment is discussed, one is often moved by the moral and humanitarian arguments put forward, until mention is made of certain crimes which cry out to Heaven for vengeance. One may talk of degrees of murder and extenuating circumstances. One remembers that in these enlightened times the reform of the criminal comes before mass revenge, but there are some crimes for which there can never be forgiveness. Such a crime was that of Jean-Baptiste Troppmann.

If ever justice was done, it was done when the blade of the guillotine fell on the neck of that wild beast. There can be no question of his guilt, his sole guilt, yet such was the spirit of the time that the public were inclined to believe his wild stories of accomplices. Troppmann was from Alsace, which with Lorraine was to pass into German hands after the war of 1870. His was not the only crime associated with that unhappy territory and there is no doubt that, in the general spy fever of the time, several of these crimes were given a political flavour. It is clear that Troppmann was the last straw in the national disillusionment towards the end of the régime. His crime seemed to announce that this was the end of law and order. Thus the people blamed the régime more than the murderer, and the destruction of the dossiers of the case under the Commune only added an air of mystery and uncertainty which persisted for many years afterwards.

The discovery of the body of Jean Kinck completed the case for the prosecution against Jean-Baptiste Troppmann, who stood accused of the murder of Madame Kinck and her six children. To the indictment could now be added the murder of the father.

On the morning of 20th September, 1869, a labourer discovered traces of fresh digging in a field about a mile from the Pantin Gate of Paris. He investigated with his pick and un-covered part of a face. He called the police, who in due course dug up the fresh bodies of a woman and five young children. There were four boys, aged five, eight, ten and thirteen, and a little girl of two. The final touch of horror was that the woman was six months advanced in pregnancy. All had been slaughtered with maniacal violence with a knife and pick-axe. The official account of the wounds inflicted, and the pitiful description of the clothing and possessions of the little victims, is a most distressing document to read. Suffice it to say that all the bodies had been terribly mutilated with the pick, as though the murderer had wanted to make certain of his work. Nevertheless, it is by no means certain that they were all dead when he buried them. The murder must have been very recent too, as the bodies were scarcely cold.

Identification was quickly established from indications on the clothing. In addition, the proprietor of the Railway Hotel at the Gare du Nord informed the police that a woman with five children had called at the hotel only the night before and had asked for Jean Kinck. They had then disappeared. The victims were identified as Madame Kinck and five of her children, who had lived up to the time of the murder at Roubaix, close to the Belgian frontier. Of the Kinck family two remained to be accounted for, the father and the eldest son Gustave, a youth of sixteen. At the time of the discovery of the murders at Pantin, they were both missing, and it was thought that Jean Kinck was the murderer or at least one of the murderers, since it was difficult to believe that the night's killing could be the work of one man.

The night of 19th September was particularly dark, with a

strong wind blowing heavy clouds across the feeble rays of the moon. Late that night, a cab drew up at the Porte de Pantin. The cabby seemed undecided about driving beyond the outskirts of Paris on such a night, but a man who was travelling inside put his head out and ordered him to drive on. In the cab, as the driver later reported, were a woman, her five children, and a young man who appeared to be a friend of the family. The young man was Jean-Baptiste Troppmann, a native of Alsace. They were all on their way to a property, which the father Jean Kinck, according to Troppmann, had purchased in the loneliest part of Pantin, and where they were to rejoin him. A strange story this, and a strange place to take a woman with five small children, tired from the recent long journey from Roubaix, so late at night.

Finally, the driver was ordered by the young man to stop at the edge of a field. Here Troppmann helped Madame Kinck to get down with the little girl and one of the small boys. He told the other three boys to stay in the cab while he went with the mother and the two children to find the father and bring him back to them. The three boys sat in the cab, and the driver got down and passed the time chatting with them. They said their friend Troppmann had brought them there to meet their father. Twenty-five minutes later Troppmann came back alone and told the three boys to get down. He informed the driver with ominous truth that it had been decided that they would all stay there, and that he could take his cab back to Paris. The driver, not a little surprised at this curious behaviour, drove off. The last he saw of the strange party was Troppmann taking the boys off into the darkness.

As we have seen, the bodies of all six were found next morning in their hurriedly dug grave. In the meantime the

66

trusted friend of the family had left for Havre, where he told chance acquaintances that he was going to try his fortune in America. Unfortunately for him, he picked up one chance acquaintance who happened to be a police informer. He was unwise enough to ask this man to assist him in obtaining false papers. While they were seated in a café, a policeman walked in and, having nothing to do, asked the furtive-looking young man his name. Troppmann did not react very naturally, and the policeman's suspicions were roused. He told Troppmann to go to the police station with him, but on the way Troppmann bolted, ran along a jetty and threw himself into the harbour. He was eventually hauled out, and it was then found that his pockets were stuffed with papers and other personal property belonging to Jean Kinck. It was thus thought at first that it was the missing Jean Kinck who had been captured, but it was soon realised, however, that this could not be Jean Kinck, the father of a family. In any case, on the 24th, Troppmann admitted his identity. The hue and cry which had followed as soon as the murders were discovered and this rapid capture naturally caused a sensation throughout France.

Having identified himself, Troppmann was faced with the problem of talking himself out of what was, to say the least, an unenviable situation. Here began the first of a series of lying statements rich in ingenuity but rather lacking in coherence. His opening story was that Jean and Gustave Kinck together murdered the wife and children, Jean having suspected his wife of adultery. In this version of what happened, Troppmann admitted his presence on the fatal field but as a helpless onlooker, even grappling with the murderers in a vain attempt to save the victims. The bottom fell out of this story when the body of Gustave Kinck was found two days later, buried close to the grave of his mother and the rest of the family. Gustave had been stabbed seven times. The heart was pierced twice, the throat was torn open, and the knife was buried up to the hilt in the body.

Undeterred by the failure of this tale, Troppmann was reduced to blaming the murders on Jean Kinck alone. He adapted his story – in fact, all the stories in this strange affair – without turning a hair. It all fitted in, because in the second version of Troppmann's story Jean Kinck also murdered his son Gustave. Troppmann had not wished to accuse Jean of this further crime out of a sense of delicacy!

When the body of Jean Kinck, murdered with home-made prussic acid from Troppmann's do-it-yourself laboratory, was found in Alsace, the second story fell flat.

Throughout the whole trial there was only one thing which could be said in Troppmann's favour; it was incredible that this mass butchery could be the work of one man and a runt-like creature like Troppmann at that. Yet, despite his unathletic appearance, he was exceptionally strong and of an animal ferocity. It is difficult to believe that a whole family could have delivered themselves with complete confidence into the hands of this killer, young enough to be the son of Jean Kinck. How had this come about?

The story begins with Troppmann's arrival in Roubaix from Alsace. He had been sent by his father to set up a textile machine. The father's factory in Alsace produced these machines, and Troppmann had already carried out one mission to Paris to supervise the erection of one such machine at Pantin, where he was later to carry out seven of the murders.

At Roubaix he had fallen in with Jean Kinck, an Alsatian like himself, who had settled in Roubaix. Kinck was a plodder who had painstakingly built up a business worth a hundred thousand francs. Kinck took Troppmann home, and there he first met his victims, Hortense, the wife, an unlettered and timid woman, and her brood of six children. The future murderer became the young friend of the family. The knock on the door in *Macbeth* could not have been more dramatic than the appearance of Jean-Baptiste Troppmann at the Kincks' front door. He was then nineteen years old, a weak-faced, unhealthy-looking creature, secretive and boastful as the mood took him. Monsieur Claude has given us a detailed description of him. He had a broad forehead and abundant chestnut hair, of which he seemed vain. Below the noble brow the rest was the face of a fiend. Large ears, a straight, hooked nose, a large upper lip on which grew what Monsieur Claude calls a nascent moustache, and unsightly teeth, in all *une physiognomie sauvage*. With this went remarkable agility and strength, which were to test many of the guards whose duty it was to keep this wild beast caged. Madame Kinck, with that instinct one so often finds in otherwise unintelligent women, dd not like him.

Jean Kinck suffered from chronic homesickness. Though he had been settled in Roubaix for thirty years, he longed for his native Alsace. This longing and the familiar sound of the dialect of his homeland must have played a big part in his attachment to Troppmann. Kinck, the self-made man, basked in the envy and admiration of his young countryman, and allowed himself to be amused and half-interested by Troppmann's romancing and ever-changing plans for making a fortune. The French do not care for Alsatians, and that doubtless threw the two of them together, the middle-aged man and the scheming boy of nineteen.

Among the hare-brained ideas which Troppmann discussed

with Kinck was a scheme for making counterfeit money. Troppmann so he said, had friends who would be ready to make over plant to him for a consideration. Kinck surprisingly listened to the plan, which Troppmann said could best be realised in their own homeland in Alsace. Troppmann knew of a place beneath the ruins of the castle of Herrenfluch where everything could be organised and the plant set up in the greatest secrecy. Talk of travelling separately to the rendezvous made the whole business mysterious and alluring. Little did Jean Kinck realise that Troppmann had his own good reasons for not being seen with him. In the end Kinck took the bait, and he and Troppmann set off for Bollwiller in Alsace by different routes. In Troppmann's pocket was a bottle of prussic acid. From Bollwiller the two travelled to Sultz, where Kinck left his luggage. Troppmann had no luggage. All he needed was the bottle of prussic acid and a bottle of wine, which he bought on the way.

From Sultz the two travellers went on foot towards Cernay on a road which passes close to the ruined castle of Herrenfluch. This was the place which Troppmann had designated as the most suitable site for setting up the counterfeit plant. Kinck was never seen alive again.

The same night Troppmann returned to his home town of Cernay. He was seen to have a new watch, plenty of money and a satisfied but very mysterious air. In the afternoon of the following day he began to write letters. Among them was one to Madame Kinck. Will she please present a cheque for five thousand five hundred francs at Kinck's bank in Roubaix and send the money to Guebwiller post office? He explained that Jean Kinck had injured his hand and he, Troppmann, was therefore writing at Kinck's dictation. It is curious how often this thin story of the injured hand crops up in trials for murder and forgery. The signature on the cheque he enclosed was not Kinck's but a close enough imitation. Apart from the injury to Kinck's hand, wrote the friend of the family, all is going well.

In due course he went to Guebwiller. Madame Kinck had carried out his instructions, and the money was there at the post office awaiting him. But the package was addressed to Jean Kinck and the postmaster was maddeningly cautious. He refused to hand over the money until Troppmann could produce a satisfactory authority. So Troppmann went away, and came back two days later with an authority apparently signed by Jean Kinck, stating that the bearer, his son Jean, could collect. But French officialdom is a peculiarly immovable object. The signature of Jean Kinck had to be registered before a notary! Troppmann returned the next day with the same paper and renewed his efforts to get the package of notes over the counter. But this time another spanner was thrown into the carefully prepared works. A distant relative of Jean Kinck happened to come into the post office. She announced, in front of the postmaster, 'I am a relative of Jean Kinck by marriage, and he has no son named Jean!' The postmaster looked even more suspicious. Troppmann tried to put the woman off with a story that he was Jean Emile Kinck, and managed to make his escape while the woman was trying to puzzle it all out.

Troppmann drove back to Cernay in his cab. He had failed. Sterner measures were called for. He took leave of his family and left for Paris, where he put up at the Railway Hotel at the Gare du Nord. He wrote again to Madame Kinck in the name of her husband. In the letter he stated that 'Troppmann has put me in the way of half a million,' and gave instructions for Gustave, armed with the proper procuration, to go to

71

Guebwiller and collect the package of money from the obstinate postmaster. He added that the whole family should then come to Paris.

So Gustave went off to Guebwiller and stayed with his aunt. Unfortunately he did not take with him the duly attested authority, which Troppmann had sent to be put in order at Roubaix at the town hall. Madame Kinck received it from the notary only after Gustave had left. She therefore sent it off to Guebwiller addressed to Gustave *poste restante*. But the poor muddle-headed Madame Kinck, worried by all the mystery and the long absence of her husband, somehow got the impression that she had addressed it to Gustave care of his aunt. This new setback in Troppmann's scheme could not be put right, as he could not guess what had happened. Gustave was afraid his father in Paris would be angry that he had left Roubaix without the document. He telegraphed to Paris after a few days, saying that he had not been able to obtain the money. Troppmann, always writing as Jean Kinck, countermanded the instruction for the whole family to come to Paris. Letters went to and fro between the harassed Madame Kinck and the impatient Troppmann. Finally, Gustave, tired of sitting at Guebwiller, wrote to his father that he was coming to Paris on 7th September. Troppmann received the news since he had registered at the hotel in the name of Jean Kinck. Troppmann met Gustave on arrival, and made him send a telegram to his mother, instructing her to come to Paris at once, bringing the children and all the family papers.

And that is all we know about Gustave until his body was dug up in the field at Pantin.

Meanwhile, Madame Kinck dressed the children in their best clothes, and on that fateful Sunday started the longest journey the poor woman had ever made in her life. This time it was a journey into death for herself and her children. Troppmann, ever busy, had been to an ironmonger's shop to buy a pick and spade. He insisted on stronger handles being fitted and called back later to collect the finished tools.

Exhausted by the long journey, Madame Kinck arrived at the hotel in Paris and inquired for Jean Kinck. She was not of course to know that the 'Jean Kinck' in the register represented the unholy person of Jean-Baptiste Troppmann. 'Jean Kinck' was out, buying certain tools as it happened, not entirely unconnected with the fate of Madame Kinck; so she went back to the station, where she thought her husband might meet the next train.

At 10.45 p.m. she was met by Troppmann, a sinister figure in a long grey coat. When she asked for her husband, Troppmann said he was awaiting them at Pantin, and they would go out there in a cab at once.

It was then that the fateful *cortège* set off, Madame with the baby girl on her lap, and the two smallest boys, one on each side of her. Opposite sat Troppmann with the other two boys. We already know how Troppmann dismissed the cab, and we can only conjecture what horror was done that night as he took the two groups into the darkness to meet the father.

If there is any doubt as to whether this crime could be the work of one man, let us remember that mother and children trusted Troppmann implicitly, and were eagerly expecting the promised reunion with husband and father. All that was needed therefore was a surprise attack and savage, unrelenting ferocity. The only one who could hope to defend herself was the mother, and she was carrying the baby in her arms. From the autopsy it was revealed that she had been stabbed many times, and was probably unconscious before she could think of defending her little ones. These could be despatched quickly or rendered silent and helpless with one or two blows with the pick. Recovering his breath, Troppmann then went back for the other three boys. One of these, when found, had had his head smashed with one blow and was partly strangled. Another was choked with a cravat, and the third was struck through the centre of the forehead with the pick. The attack was clearly so sudden and unexpected that none had been able to make any defence, except the little Alfred, aged five, who was killed with his mother, and whose hands were cut with the knife as he tried to ward off the blows.

The good friend of the family then interred the six bodies – dead or dying, it mattered not to him – where they were discovered the next day. Taking the papers and the money, which Madame Kinck had brought with her, Troppmann left, and our next meeting with him is at Havre. Thus the picture is complete; the father poisoned and buried in his native earth of Alsace, the eldest son stabbed and buried in the same field where the rest of the family had been slaughtered.

Troppmann had been fished out of the water at Havre and taken to the local hospital. It is as well to mention that Troppmann did his best to drown the dock worker who had dived into the water to save him. The struggle in the water prevented him from disposing of the incriminating documents he was carrying and they were found on him when he was undressed at the hospital. As we may well imagine, Monsieur Claude went up to Havre at once. He was having no nonsense from this half-drowned rat wrapped in a blanket in a hospital bed. He had him dressed at once for removal to Paris. Troppmann's arrival, carefully guarded, at the railway station, was

74

met by a menacing crowd, who would most certainly have finished off the drowning job if they could have got their hands on him. He travelled in a first-class carriage to Paris, Monsieur Claude seated at his right hand. There were crowds at every stop, as at a Royal progress. At Rouen the crowd tried to storm the train and tear down the blinds on the carriage windows, and the train was delayed for twenty minutes before order was restored.

In Paris crowds had been gathering round the Gare Saint-Lazare for two days. There is no doubt he would have been torn to pieces had he not been spirited away by cab from a private exit. More detectives followed in another cab. Not without difficulty the two cabs eventually arrived at the morgue. Monsieur Claude says that at the station in Paris Troppmann was on the point of collapse. His legs almost gave way under him and, as Monsieur Claude reports, his complexion was more than pale; it was green with fear. Having got nothing out of him during the journey from Havre, Claude decided to confront him with the bodies without delay, in the hope he would break down and confess.

In the mortuary the six unclothed bodies were laid out. The registrar of the morgue had signed a simple receipt for them;

Received six bodies, sent by the *Commissaire* of Pantin.

20th September, 1869

What had been a happy young family, dressed in their best clothes and carrying the little toys and parcels of food found with their remains, only a day or two before, was now a row of horribly mutilated bodies on a mortuary slab. Knowing how they were killed, it is not necessary for us to examine each body in detail. Troppmann was unmoved when the *juge d'instruction* asked, 'Do you recognise these bodies?'

75

Troppmann stepped forward, scratching his ear like a cat, as Claude reports. He shrugged his shoulders and replied without emotion, 'Yes, that's Madame Kinck, that's Emile, that's Henri, that's Alfred, that's Achille and that's little Marie.' He pointed to each one as he spoke without deigning to take his hat off. This, for Monsieur Claude, was the last straw.

It was not until six days after the death of Madame Kinck and her five children that the body of Gustave, her eldest, was found at Pantin buried not far from the rest of the family. He had been stabbed in the throat with a kitchen knife which the murderer had left in the wound. In addition he had received blows with a pick in the chest and in the back of the neck. It was obvious that he had put up a good fight for his life. So the seventh corpse duly arrived at the morgue.

Troppmann, now in the Prison of Mazas, was at once pushed into a cab by Monsieur Claude to be driven to the morgue, though he was told he was being taken to the *Conciergerie.* The blinds of the cab were lowered so that Troppmann could not see where he was being taken. Claude again was trying sudden confrontation with the corpse to see if he could get an admission out of Troppmann. It was a surprise for him when he was suddenly shown the body of Gustave and for a moment he tried to cover his face with a handkerchief. 'Take that handkerchief away!' shouted the *juge d'instruction,* 'Do you recognise this body?' 'Yes,' replied Troppmann, 'it's Gustave.' 'And it's you who murdered him!' said the *juge.* 'No! It was his father!' said Troppmann.

The *juge* then pointed out that Troppmann had stated that the father and son had committed the other murders. How then had one of the murderers suddenly become a victim? Then Troppmann produced his next card. 'It was probably because his father killed him to prevent him from ever revealing such an abominable crime!' Troppmann accompanied Claude back to the Mazas prison without saying another word. In the meantime the fatal field at Pantin had been trampled by a hundred thousand Parisians into a mire in which cartwheels stuck fast.

Monsieur Claude rightly guessed that the body of Jean Kinck – for it was highly doubtful if he was still alive – would be found in Alsace, but it was not until November that his perseverance was rewarded.

By that time Troppmann had quite a problem on his hands to explain away the murder of the whole family. To the questions: Who was last seen with Jean Kinck? Who was last seen with Gustave? Who was last seen with Madame Kinck and the children? Who bought the tools? Who registered under the name of Jean Kinck at the hotel? Who tried to get the money at Guebwiller? Who had Jean Kinck's papers in his possession?, the answer is always 'Troppmann!'

We now come to the next story fabricated by the ever-inventive Troppmann. He had accomplices. This came about in the following way. He had surprised three men committing a robbery at Cernay in 1868. They later offered him money if he would keep silent. Being a man of principle, he had naturally refused, but he had kept in touch with them. He told Jean Kinck that they were the friends who were prepared to sell the counterfeiting plant. This was complicated by another story in which Troppmann was to lure Kinck to Cernay to be robbed by these three men, after which the spoils would be shared with Troppmann. He thus met Kinck at Bollwiller, and with the three robbers set off. One of these accomplices handed Kinck a bottle of wine from which he drank and fell dead. The murderer had put into the wine some of the prussic acid which

Troppmann had given him months before to poison a dog. Then, on the instructions of this man, Troppmann sent a cheque to Roubaix to be cashed with a request that the money be sent to Guebwiller. In the midst of all this, Troppmann added the interesting information that one of the accomplices had gone off to Mulhouse to get married, but that he cut short his honeymoon to rejoin Troppmann and the other two, now in Paris. One of these had been engaged in digging a grave at Pantin! With a First, Second and Third murderer and now a Gravedigger, the whole story was becoming quite Shakespearian. The accomplice who had killed Jean Kinck then killed Gustave on his arrival in Paris. About this time Madame Kinck had been persuaded to come to Paris. She and the children had been taken out to Pantin and handed over *'comme c'était convenu entre nous'* to the three accomplices. Troppmann tried in vain to prevent the murder of the younger children, bravely cutting his own hand in the struggle. Nevertheless, he collected the three little boys and handed them over to the three men, who despatched them at once.

Curiously enough, the three alleged murderers, after all this toil and trouble, allowed Troppmann to take away all the papers and valuables which Madame Kinck was carrying. In another story he admitted having killed Jean Kinck and rambled on to problems of electro-chemistry, which he had studied and which gave him access to prussic acid, an important ingredient in his counterfeiting process. Furthermore, there were hints about overhearing plans for declaring war on France in the spy-ridden, Franco-German corner of France near his home. Even the wily Monsieur Claude gives some credence to an international political background to the Troppmann affair. Claude had had his fingers burned in another criminal case and had even been assaulted in Alsace. He was therefore inclined to see German spies under every table. I cannot imagine any espionage organisation having anything to do with an unreliable character like Troppmann, who one moment would be discussing international secrets and the next would announce, as he did, that he had discovered some gold and silver mines in Alsace! To sum up, Troppmann's defence is a story with as many holes as a fishnet.

Pressed to name his accomplices, he withdrew into a dignified and mysterious silence. All he would say, when pressed further, was that Jean Kinck had entrusted to him a letter addressed to the three counterfeiters. This letter Troppmann delivered and Kinck received a reply, which he kept in a pocket-book with a copy of the original letter. The pocket-book was given to Troppmann by the man who poisoned Jean Kinck. Here we may recall that he had admitted killing Jean Kinck himself. Also in this pocket-book were two blank cheques and some notes on the manufacture of counterfeit money. Troppmann then buried the pocket-book in a secret place known only to him. If he were taken to Alsace, he could point out the exact spot to the police. But the police were not going to give Troppmann a chance to escape *en route,* and the pocket-book despite searches based on plans supplied by Troppmann, has not yet been found.

Although valiantly defended by the famous advocate Lachaud, who based his arguments on the theory that this mass murder could not possibly be the work of one man and that there was substance in the story of the accomplices, Troppmann was found guilty. The trial was a fashionable spectacle, to be compared only with the trial of Landru much later. The carnival atmosphere continued in the buffet supper given in the rooms of the Governor of the prison of La Roquette during Troppmann's last night on earth. Among the guests were Victorien Sardou, the Russian writer Turgenev, Maxime du Camp, Albert Wolff and of course, Monsieur Claude, *Chef de la Sûreté*!

While the wines and good food were circulating, Troppmann was sleeping soundly downstairs in the condemned cell. At six o'clock in the morning, Monsieur Claude announced to him that his appeal had been rejected together with his plea to the Emperor. He was told that the time of expiation had come and that he must be courageous. He did not reply. Then he was asked, 'Do you admit your guilt in the crimes for which you have been condemned?' He replied, 'Yes, but I did not strike the blows myself.' Claude then asked, 'Will you reveal the names of your accomplices?' Troppmann firmly replied, *'Je ne le veux pas!'*

They took off his strait-jacket, for he had had to be confined like a wild animal, and strapped him ready for the guillotine. At the foot of the machine, he embraced the priest and said in his appalling Alsatian accent, 'Tell Monsieur Claude that I persist . . .'

Until then he had been more or less composed, but he began to struggle as he was dragged to the guillotine. He tried to get his head beyond the retaining board where the knife comes down. He raged and fought and bit the hand of the executioner. As the knife fell, his head had twisted round, and he must have seen the blade as it dropped. As the head fell, two men rushed forward, dipped their handkerchiefs in the blood and fled into the crowd. Who were they? Perhaps the accomplices?

In those confused times just before the fall of the Second

Empire, all kinds of theories were put forward to solve the mystery behind the Troppmann case. The fact that Kinck and Troppmann were both from Alsace prompted stories of espionage and suppressed evidence. It was also suggested that there was an immoral association between Kinck and Troppmann. Many people continued to believe in the existence of accomplices; but the papers had been destroyed and the case could never be re-opened. Of one thing we can be sure; justice was done. All the roads in this case lead to Troppmann, and we can view his departure with dry eyes.

Returning to the question of the abolition of capital punishment, it must be admitted that the execution of Troppmann has not prevented other monstrous crimes. But is there anyone who can plead clemency for such a monster? He was not a deprived child. This was not a crime prompted by passion or starvation. He was quite sane. All one can feel is that he was a proof that evil is a real, tangible thing. Though he was sane, he would have had to be kept in a strait-jacket had he been reprieved. He was a coiled spring, a wild beast ready to strike with lightning fury at any moment, as he did on that dreadful night in the field at Pantin. Would it have been right to condemn a series of people to guard him for perhaps another fifty years?

When we read of the careers and fate of men such as Troppmann, many of us – especially those of us who have children – cannot help thinking, apart from the wrong done to the victims of their crimes, of the sorrow and misery they bring to their own families. The Troppmanns and Heaths and Kramers of this world were once dearly-cherished babies and then bright little boys, in whom the pride and hopes of their parents were centred. Yet those parents were condemned to see

81

their children grow into universally reviled monsters and to live through the hour of their execution. As a change from the surfeit of evil we have just witnessed, I include a simple little ghost story which I translated from the German of the Brothers Grimm. It might well be called 'The Criminals Who Never Were' but the Brothers Grimm have entitled it

THE LITTLE OLD MOTHER

IN A GREAT CITY ONE EVENING A LITTLE OLD MOTHER WAS SITTING ALONE in her room. She was thinking how first she had lost her husband, then both her children and one by one all her relations, even her last friend, and now was left entirely alone. Deep in her heart she was sad and most of all she mourned the loss of her sons, for which she reproached God in her grief. So she sat quietly, lost in herself, when suddenly she heard the bell for the first morning service. She was amazed that she had sat the whole night through with her sorrow. However, she lit her lamp and made her way to church.

When she entered, it was already lighted up not, as usual, with candles but with a twilight glow. It was filled with people and all the seats were occupied. As the old mother came to her customary place, it was no longer free and the whole bench was packed. And when she looked at the people, she saw that they were none other than her dead relatives; there they sat in their old-fashioned clothes but with dead-white faces. They neither sang nor spoke but throughout the church there sounded a quiet humming and lamentation.

Then one of her female relatives stood up, came over to the old mother and said to her: 'There, look towards the altar and you will see your sons.' The old lady looked and saw both her children; one was hanging on a gallows, the other lay broken on the wheel. Again the woman spoke: 'You see, that is what would have happened to them if they had lived and if God had not taken them to Himself as innocent children.'

The old lady went trembling back to her house and thanked God on her knees that He had dealt better with her than she could have understood; and on the third day she lay down and died.

CHAPTER EIGHT

THE STRANGE CASE OF DR BUCK RUXTON

AMONG CRIMES OF MURDER AND MUTILATION, THE CASE OF DR BUCK Ruxton is unique, primarily because the manner of mutilation provided a problem in anatomical reconstruction never encountered before. That problem was solved and the murderer was convicted and sentenced to death on evidence, which Mr Justice Singleton rightly said could leave no doubt in the mind of anyone. Rarely has a murder indictment been put more clearly and fairly to a jury and never before has such skill and knowledge of forensic medicine been employed to bring a murderer to justice. Apart from the enormous mass of scientific evidence which was assembled at the trial to demonstrate conclusively the guilt of the prisoner, his own behaviour betrayed him almost from the beginning. Nevertheless the case remains a mystery. This mystery lies not only in the strange personality of Dr Buck Ruxton himself but in the actual circumstances in which the murders were committed. No one to this day knows exactly how or why he took the lives of his wife and Mary Rogerson that night in 1935.

Were it not for the tragedy and horror which surrounds this case, Dr Buck Ruxton would present almost a comic figure. He could easily have joined Tommy Handley's gallery of ITMA characters. His frantic and unconvincing lying, his painful sentimentality, his frequent outbursts of temper and fits of weeping, together with his penny novelette and babu English do not suggest the killer at all, still less the cold-blooded butcher. Even his adopted name smacks more of the Wild West novel or boys' detective story than of real life.

He was born in Bombay, his name originally being Bukhtyar Rustomji Ratanji Hakim. This was abbreviated to Buck Hakim and later to Buck Ruxton. He almost belonged to the 'failed BA' class. In fact he had failed in the examination for the

Fellowship of the Royal College of Surgery of Edinburgh, though he was a Bachelor of Medicine of the Universities of Bombay and London and a Bachelor of Surgery of Bombay. This latter qualification was to stand him in good stead. Despite these degrees, however, he could scarcely be numbered among the more eminent of the followers of Aesculapius.

We find him at the age of thirty-one established in practice in a shabby double-fronted house next to a cinema in Dalton Square, Lancaster. He then had a wife and one child. It might be added that, although his wife was referred to as such throughout the trial, it was by courtesy only, since there is no trace of any marriage. Mrs Ruxton, as we shall continue to call her, was born Isabella Kerr and was married to a Dutchman called Van Ess. This marriage was dissolved and she went to live with Ruxton in London in 1928.

It was by no means a happy ménage even from the beginning. Their life together consisted of a series of violent quarrels and passionate reconciliations. Ruxton was a man of unbalanced emotions and morbid suspicions. He had fits of incredible and probably unjustified jealousy, since Mrs Ruxton can never have been a raging beauty. She was rather a horse-faced masculine type of woman with thick ankles, these physiological details being confirmed later in the pitiful reassembly of her remains by the Faculties of Forensic Medicine of the Universities of Glasgow and Edinburgh.

By 1934, they had three children and the frantic scenes of jealousy with threats, abuse and violence continued to the point that the police had to be called in on several occasions. Such scenes usually ended with the little doctor in tears of self-pity and remorse.

This instability of character and erratic behaviour may conceivably have arisen from the fact that he was not legally married to this European woman and that, as an Indian, he suffered from a feeling of inferiority. His English at times was almost babu. He used dramatic expressions with comic irrelevance, which suggests that his education was rather a patchy and superficial affair. After the murders, his behaviour was a mixture of wild panic and violent indignation that anyone dared suspect him. At times he must almost have convinced himself that his wife and maid had really run away and left him and not been murdered and cut up in the bathroom at Dalton Square.

His curious mentality is best exemplified in his carefully removing any identification marks from the bodies. It did not occur to him that, in cutting out a bunion on his wife's foot and in peeling the vaccination marks off her arm, he was only drawing attention to these peculiarities.

Nevertheless, this unbalanced, nervy little man spent eight or nine hours dismembering the bodies of his wife and maid in a tiny bathroom, while his children were asleep in the same house. He came from this slaughterhouse to prepare food for his children in the morning. He was capable of performing a job requiring considerable anatomical skill and physical endurance, which would have daunted a mediaeval hangman. But let us look at the sequence of events.

In 1934, the Ruxton household consisted of Buck Ruxton, his wife and three children and Mary Rogerson, the maid, a girl of twenty. Among the other characters of this tragedy were Mrs Curwen, Mrs Oxley and Mrs Smith, charwomen who attended at various times to do the cleaning.

Mrs Ruxton and the maid were last seen, by anyone other than Dr Ruxton, on Saturday, 14th September 1935. It is now clear that, during the night of 14/15th September, they were murdered by Dr Ruxton. A fortnight later, the dismembered and mutilated remains of two human beings were discovered in Gardenholme Linn, a stream which runs near Moffat in Dumfriesshire, below a bridge on the Moffat-Edinburgh road. Gardenholme Linn is a hundred and ten miles from Lancaster, roughly a three-hour drive.

There were four bundles, one containing two upper arms and four pieces of flesh. The second contained two thigh bones, two legs and nine pieces of flesh. There were seventeen pieces of flesh in the third bundle and in the fourth the chest portion of a human torso and two legs. In addition, two heads, a thigh bone, two forearms with hands and various pieces of flesh and skin were found scattered below the bridge.

The heads presented a peculiarly horrible spectacle. The ears, eyes, nose, lips and skin of the faces had been removed; certain teeth had been extracted, apparently after death; and most of the scalp had been removed in each case.

Unusually heavy rains about that time had washed the remains down to the place where they were discovered, rather sooner no doubt than the perpetrator of the crime had anticipated. Later, various additional pieces of flesh were recovered. Early in October, a left foot was found near the Carlisle-Glasgow road, south of Moffat, and in November a right forearm and hand were discovered by the roadside half a mile from Gardenholme Linn. It was obvious from an examination of the remains that the person responsible for the dismemberment and mutilation had some expert anatomical and medical knowledge. The bodies had been skilfully dismembered by cutting through the joints with a knife. The removal of parts of the body which might have given some indication of the cause of death, also pointed to more than lay knowledge and skill.

After their disappearance, Dr Ruxton reported his wife and maid as missing from home. During the period shortly after the murders, he behaved so foolishly and suspiciously that it is surprising that no charge was preferred against him until 13th October, when he was charged with the murder of Mary Rogerson. On 5th November he was charged with the murder of Mrs Ruxton. It must be remembered however that the identification of the bodies was an extremely difficult problem. In fact, one body was thought at first – to Ruxton's great relief – to be that of a man, so it had to be proved conclusively that the remains found at Gardenholme Linn were indeed those of Mrs Ruxton and Mary Rogerson. In a murder trial a body has to be produced, unless there is direct evidence of the killing, and it has to be the body of the person alleged to have been murdered. But from the moment those two women were killed up to the time the identity of the bodies had been established, Dr Ruxton went about industriously fixing the noose round his neck in his own way.

One can imagine the scene shortly after midnight on the night of 14/15th September. The house was suddenly quiet, a dreadful ticking-of-the-clock quiet with only faint sounds coming from the street outside. A few moments before, one may conjecture, there had been the noise of a violent quarrel with the doctor shouting accusations of infidelity at his wife, she defending herself and possibly the maid vainly trying to help her mistress. Then the paroxysm of rage, the blows, the cries and finally, silence. The children were asleep in another room. Dr Ruxton was alone with two bodies. His feet were now firmly set on the road to the gallows in Strangeways Prison.

He had eight, perhaps nine hours before the milk girl made her call, before the newspaper boy rang the bell, before a patient was due for a minor operation he had promised to perform. But Dr Ruxton had a major operation before him, the biggest job in his whole career.

He had to undress the bodies, drag them to the small bathroom and prepare his instruments. We know that he had to put the bodies in water in the bath to assist with the draining of the blood. The bath was found later to have overflowed and a witness said that it was stained almost to the edge.

To dismember a body in a dissecting room with all the necessary equipment to hand is no small task. Ruxton had two bodies to deal with and all he had in the way of equipment was a knife with interchangeable blades. He had no saw and all disarticulation was carried out by cutting through the joints with the knife. In addition to dissecting the bodies into conveniently portable parts, he had to remove the skin of the head; the eyes and other identifiable features; he had to extract the teeth and remove finger tips to avoid identification of the prints. But he left the finger tips on one body, the prints of which corresponded with prints found later on objects at Dalton Square.

So he worked hour after hour, calculating all eventualities, trying to anticipate the findings of a police doctor if the remains were discovered, planning his journeys to the place selected for concealment, working out a timetable and all the time cutting and slicing in a reeking shambles. Then, in the midst of this nightmare task, he did the one thing all doctors fear in a dissection. He cut his hand badly. The chances of fatal infection were considerable, but imagine his situation. He couldn't stop. He had to wrap the profusely bleeding cut, which extended across his fingers, and continue working, cutting and severing until the frightful work was finished.

Witnesses who testified that he looked like death afterwards can hardly be doubted. But even then, the job was not finished. There was the burning of the clothes, the clearing up, the packing of the remains in newspapers – one of which, a slip edition for the Lancaster area – was to tighten the noose even more firmly round his neck. Then there was the journey to be worked out, the loading of the car, the purchase of petrol, the dumping of the parcels and the quick return to Lancaster to fit in with the timetable of his story.

This was no premeditated murder. It was committed in a fit of rage, so all arrangements for the concealment of the bodies had to be improvised. People who called had to be put off; rooms, otherwise left open, had to be locked; and the children had to be taken away on the following day.

From then onwards, Ruxton told one improbable story after another. His wife had run away with another man. His wife had taken Mary Rogerson away, as the girl was pregnant and was to have an abortion. His wife had gone off to open a betting office. Then he gave away a blood-soaked suit. He later went back to ask for the return of the suit after insisting that the name tab should be cut out and burned in his presence!

It must have been obvious from his first visit to the police station that he was guilty. His accounts of his movements were lying and conflicting. He asked various people to say they had or had not seen him on given dates, all in a crazy attempt to hold his flimsy timetable together. He tore up stair-carpets, stripped walls and pulled down curtains which were stained. The amazing thing was that the three ministering charwomen saw nothing unduly suspicious in his actions or in the condition of the house at the time. It was only at the trial that their evidence was to be so significant. He had a bonfire in the yard and left identifiable articles of clothing lying about. He gave some of his wife's clothes away, surely an indication that he knew he would never see her again. In fact he could not have demonstrated his guilt more clearly. But the bodies had to be identified beyond doubt and that was by no means easy.

Among the many experiments carried out by the experts were super-impositions of enlarged photographs of Mrs Ruxton and Mary Rogerson, taken during life, on to photographs of the skulls. They were found to be curiously exact in the way they fitted. Shoes belonging to the women were tried on casts of the feet. A dentist made a denture and fitted it in one of the skulls. It was similar to one which had been made for Mrs Ruxton before her death. Even the life cycle of the maggots infesting the remains was studied to assist in establishing the approximate date of death.

In the examination and reassembly of the remains, there was one mystery which has not been solved. It was the mystery of the Cyclops eye. The following passage occurs in De Quincey's *The English Mail-Coach,* Section II, 'The Vision of Sudden Death': 'But what was Cyclops doing here? Had the medical men recommended northern air, or how? I collected, from such explanations as he volunteered, that he had an interest at stake in some suit-at-law now pending at Lancaster.' The association of Cyclops with a suit-at-law at Lancaster so many years before is a most curious coincidence. A Cyclops eye, a monstrous malformation in which two eyes are almost fused into one, was found among the remains. The judge, in his summing-up, expressed the view that its appearance was accidental and had no significance in the case. But, as De Quincey asked in another connexion, what was Cyclops doing here? This particular type of malformation occurs more often in pigs and sheep than in human beings. Unfortunately it was not possible to say definitely if it was of human or animal origin. The monstrous eye which was found was in rather a better state of preservation than the rest of the remains. The double optic nerve had been cut in a very clean manner and did not appear to have rotted away from other tissue, as one might have expected. There are two suggested explanations for the presence of this specimen. If the eye could have been proved to be human, it might have been argued by the defence that it was part of a monstrous birth. It will be remembered that one of Dr Ruxton's explanations for his wife's absence was that she had taken Mary Rogerson away for an illegal operation. The alleged abortionist could have killed Mary Rogerson in the course of the operation and then have murdered Mrs Ruxton as a witness against him. Whether such a notion had entered the panic-stricken mind of Dr Ruxton we shall never know. The other possibility is that Ruxton possessed a preserved specimen of a Cyclops eye. He was known to have had an interest in ophthalmology. It would have been preserved in formalin and, in the absence of any other supply, he may have poured it over the human remains and emptied the specimen itself among them. Had it been known that he did own such a specimen, it would have furnished yet another link between Gardenholme Linn and the house in Dalton Square, Lancaster.

Eventually the case for the Crown was complete and the trial at Manchester Assizes took eleven days. Ruxton was called and, in the course of a lengthy cross-examination frequently burst into tears. He constantly referred to his wife as 'my Belle', 'my poor Bella' and 'Isabel'. The unfortunate maid was 'my poor Mary' or 'my Mary'. His children were 'my little mites'. In reply to one question, he said, 'My mentality thinks in French and I have to translate into English everything you are asking me,' whatever that might mean. When asked what he did when he cut his hand – as he said he had done when opening a tin of peaches for the children – he replied, 'I just wrapped a handkerchief round my hand carelessly – haphazardly – as a first intention.' Asked if he had referred to 'my little maid', he answered, 'No, it is the great ambiguity of the English language. I never used the words "little maid". I did say "my little mites", my children. Why should I use the words "my little maid?" What purpose was there in my mind?' He then added, 'Belle has often rebuked me for saying "my Mary", but that is a French expression.' So this poor little muddler went on, losing himself in meaningless words and seemingly unaware of the danger in which he stood.

The jury were absent for just over an hour. There could be no doubt about the verdict. The judge asked him if he had anything to say why sentence of death should not be passed according to law. Ruxton then made the following incredible statement: 'Subject to the point that I be allowed to appeal, in the administration of justice. I submit to Your Lordship and the jury. I want to thank everybody for the patience and fairness of my trial. I have never attempted to pass any special restrictions. I should like to hear whatever His Lordship has to say about it.' He heard. It was the sentence of death.

And so, with this last incomprehensible statement, Dr Buck Ruxton departed this life.

What drove him to these murders? What caused him to destroy with such savagery his wife and the harmless, simple-minded maid? He was very fond of his children and there is no doubt that he was attached to his wife. He spoke kindly of his maid in his evidence and it is obvious that she was almost a member of the family. It is true he had a quarrel with his wife only a week before, when he accused her on no grounds whatever of having an illicit love affair with a young man called Edmondson. This and her absence in Blackpool, whence she had returned on that fatal night of 14th September, probably occasioned that last violent scene, as a result of which Mrs Ruxton met her death. It can only be conjectured that he killed her in a fit of rage and then murdered the maid, who may have been a witness of the crime.

As they say in Dr Ruxton's adopted county, there's nowt so queer as folk!

CHAPTER NINE

THE MAN WHO BOUGHT A TRAM

ALMOST EVERY DAY OF HIS LIFE, ALPHONSE WENT TO THE *ETOILE DU NORD*, which was his favourite café, for a beer. There he would sit, looking out at the stream of busy Brussels life flowing by.

He knew the *patron* and indeed most of the other customers, as the Belgians are very regular in their habits, both as regards the beer they drink and the cafés they frequent. That was why he began to notice the two men, who had taken to coming in every day at about the same time as himself. They were strangers to begin with, but what caught his attention was the curious ritual which accompanied their beer drinking. One would come in, sit down at the table next to that of Alphonse and order a beer. A few minutes later, the other man would appear and a second beer would be ordered. Then the newcomer would take out a canvas bag heavy with small change. He would bang it on the table and untie the string at the top of the bag. He would solemnly count out the contents of the bag, which was full of one- and five-franc pieces. The total would usually be well over a thousand francs, sometimes as much as fifteen hundred. He would then work out ten per cent, transfer the amount to his pocket, put the balance back in the bag and hand it to the first man, who gave him a receipt for the amount. They would then finish their beer and go off in different directions.

This routine went on day after day and Alphonse became more and more intrigued. He wondered if they were bookmakers or street traders, but they did not look that type. It began to worry Alphonse and he even started to interest himself in the daily fluctuations in the takings. He simply could not help observing every detail of the proceedings.

Then one day, only one of the men turned up. He had his beer, nodded to Alphonse in a casual way and eventually went out. Next day, he was alone again. He said a *bonjour* to Alphonse and somehow they got into conversation. 'What has happened to your friend?' asked Alphonse. 'Oh, he has taken a couple of days' holiday at the coast,' replied the man. He added that he would be back again on the morrow for what he called 'the collection'. Alphonse could restrain his curiosity no longer. 'Excuse me, but I can't help noticing this curious transaction of yours every day. I have been wondering what business you are engaged in,' said Alphonse. The Belgians are not so inhibited as the English and are not ashamed to ask one another's business. 'Well, you'd never guess in a thousand years,' said the man. 'As a matter of fact, I own one of the Brussels trams. My friend is a conductor and every day he brings me the takings. I give him ten per cent for his trouble and altogether I make a pretty good living out of it.' 'But that's impossible!' said Alphonse, 'The tramways are publicly owned!' 'That is true,' said the man, 'but nevertheless I own one tram. It is a W-tram, one of those which goes to Wemmel, and I get every franc which is taken in fares, less of course the ten per cent, which I pay to the conductor to ensure his honesty. Sometimes I travel all day on my own tram just to be doubly sure that I am getting my rights.' 'But how did you come to acquire a tram?' asked Alphonse, who could scarcely believe this incredible story.

'Well,' said the man, 'it was like this. I once owned a piece of land near Wemmel when the line was extended. But the line could not be extended without cutting through my piece of land. The tramways people wanted to buy the land but I did not want to sell. Why, do you know that piece of land had been in my family since the time of Philip II and we had a charter to say so. I was not going to sell that for a few thousand francs just to suit the tram people. Now my land was so

situated that they could not very well go round it. They just
had to have my land, so I could dictate my own terms. Then I
had an idea. I said I would sell my land for a tram. Of course
they were dumbfounded. It was unheard of. Will you have
another beer, by the way?' Alphonse accepted this courtesy,
anxious to know the rest of the story. 'Well,' continued the
man, 'negotiations went on and I remained quite obstinate. The
tram people held meeting after meeting. The contract for the
extension of the tramway had been given out and time was
money. Finally, to cut a long story short, they agreed to lease
me a tram with its earnings, for twenty years. So I am being
quite handsomely paid for my piece of land. Every day, as you
see, I get the takings or the collection as we call it. Of course
the whole transaction has to be kept secret and that is why I
receive the money as I do. I get a ticket issue statement from the
tramways as a check on the money which the conductor brings
me. He doesn't know that, but I like to be sure. What I am
telling you is in the strictest confidence, of course, and I hope
you will respect it.' 'Yes,' said Alphonse, flattered by the man's
trust in him, 'you may count on me to keep it to myself.'

Alphonse still continued to take his beer at the *Etoile du
Nord* and next day and on succeeding days the routine of
handing over the tram's takings went on. Sometimes he had a
beer with the owner of the tram and the conductor and they
talked of many things. Then, one day, after the conductor had
gone, the owner of the tram said he was shortly going away to
the Congo. He had been offered a very good job there, but he
was very worried, as he did not know what to do about the
income from the tram. He ventured to consult Alphonse, as he
had by this time learned that Alphonse was head bookkeeper in
an important trading company so he appealed to him as an

experienced business-man. He could of course entrust someone to collect the daily takings on his behalf and bank it or transfer it to the Congo, but how could he feel certain that the agent would not find some way of deceiving him? The only alternative was to sell his interest in the tram, but who on earth would buy a tram? The tramways people would not agree to a transfer and he would have to do it as a private transaction. There he left the problem and Alphonse said he would think it over and see if he could suggest anything, though the man said very kindly that he did not wish to burden Alphonse with his private worries.

Alphonse gave a lot of thought to this curious dilemma over the weekend. Alphonse was a bachelor, who led a very quiet life. His tastes were simple. He spent very little money and in the course of many years of hard work, he had quite a large savings bank account against his old age.

As he strolled through the *Bois de la Cambre* that Sunday afternoon, he could not help comparing his own uneventful existence with that of people who owned trams and went off to the Congo as if it were a trip to Ostend. Then he thought what fun it would be to own a tram and collect the fares every day of one's life!

The next day he met his new-found friend at the *Etoile du Nord*. After the conductor had gone, the tram owner came back to the problem of what he was going to do with his tram when he went off to the Congo at the end of the month. Alphonse suggested that the best solution would be to sell the interest in the tram to another private individual. 'Yes,' said the man, 'that would be a good idea, but who is going to buy a tram? I would most certainly be willing to cede my rights for a lump sum but to whom? Would you buy a tram from me?' 'Well,' replied

Alphonse, 'it depends on what you want for it. I am half-tempted to invest my savings in your tram, if it could be made over to me.' 'I must think it over,' said the man and 'I'll let you know tomorrow.'

When he turned up the following day, the man had a sheaf of papers, some of them headed 'Tramways de Bruxelles', and an old charter with a seal on it, which had all manner of endorsements on it including the rubber stamp of the 'Tramways de Bruxelles'. It was impossible to read the charter, as it was in sixteenth-century Flemish and in very crabbed writing. But nevertheless on the headed paper, dated ten years before, it stated quite clearly that the 'Tramways de Bruxelles' ceded one tram, to wit No 453754, to one Ernest Denoble for a period of twenty years in consideration of his making over to them the parcel of land situate at such and such plus all manner of other lawyer's jargon. It confirmed his rights to the fares, to be disposed of as he should think fit.

Monsieur Denoble, for that was the man's name, said that on an average he took five thousand francs a week. In a year this made a quarter of a million francs. There was still a period of ten years of the contract to go. Of course, he was candid enough to explain, all kinds of things might happen. There might be strikes or perhaps a change-over to trolley-buses. There was bad weather to consider and power failures and so on but on the whole it was a steady income and in the long run held the likelihood of a large profit. He had thought it over and would sell his tram by private covenant for one and a half million francs.

Now Alphonse had almost two million francs in the bank. What with his inheritance from his father plus his savings, he could certainly raise a million and a half in cash. Over ten years, all being well, that could turn into two and a half million. He decided to delay one more day to think it over.

Finally, he made up his mind. He would do it. He would own his own tram! So the next day, after the conductor had handed over his takings to Monsieur Denoble, he signed an agreement by which, in consideration of the payment of one and a half million francs, Ernest Denoble made over his interest in Brussels tram No 453754 and all his rights to the fares taken on the said tram to Alphonse Lebrun. The signatures were witnessed by the conductor and the *patron* of the *Etoile du Nord*. Alphonse handed over a large envelope containing a million and a half francs and received in exchange a copy of the agreement and all the relevant papers, including the charter of Philip II. He agreed to go to Melsbroek on the following Saturday to see Monsieur Denoble off to Elisabethville.

The next day, Alphonse sat at his usual place in the *Etoile du Nord* and sure enough the conductor arrived and, after deducting his own ten per cent, paid over a sum of eleven hundred francs. But on the day after that, the conductor did not turn up. In fact he never visited the *Etoile du Nord* again. As to Monsieur Denoble, he must have missed his plane to Elisabethville, as he was not at Melsbroek when the flight was called.

At last, in despair Alphonse called at the Head Office of the 'Tramways de Bruxelles' to make enquiries about the functioning of tram No 453754. I am afraid I must chronicle that roars of unsympathetic laughter are still echoing round the walls of that institution, and Alphonse has a reproachful look in his eye whenever he sees a Wemmel tram pass.

CHAPTER TEN

THE HYENA AND THE FEMALE CYCLOPS

WE ARE BACK AGAIN IN THE GOTHIC WORLD OF MONSIEUR CLAUDE AND his sinister inspectors of the Paris *Sûreté.* These *limiers* or bloodhounds, as he chose to call them, are usually referred to by nicknames. Thair appearance as well as their bizarre designations are a far cry from the highly respectable Inspector Goss or Chief Ironside of our television screens. One was called Lynx-Eye, another Zinc-Collar and the hero of our present story was known as Requin or the Shark. 'He had all the qualities of a shark silently biding his time. With his hollow, greenish cheeks, his eyes which shone in the dark, he had the patience of the wild animal poised to seize its prey. His flair for the reek of blood, for the scent of a dead body was a precious resource in the pursuit of crime.' Thus Monsieur Claude on one of his principal aides!

For some months in the La Villette quarter of Paris in the year 1872, scarcely a week passed without corpses, male and female, being found in the Saint-Martin canal. All bore marks of violence. They proved to be mainly young workers from local factories. The men had usually been stabbed in the chest while the women's bodies had been mutilated in other ways. All had been robbed and the evidence showed that the murders were the work of expert criminals.

Monsieur Claude decided that this was a job for Requin, who was at once sent off to set up a flying squad near the pont de Flandre to investigate the crimes. He was no sooner installed than he was able to report one more; the body of one Becker, a worker of American origin who had been employed in a saw-mills at La Villette. He had last been seen giving a party to celebrate his departure for his own country. He had sent his bags to the station before the party, which was held in a low tavern haunted by dock workers and down-and-outs. This rather unsalubrious company had been roistering till three o'clock in the morning when a number left with their host ostensibly to see him home. He was seen no more, though this occasioned little comment, since it was known that he was leaving France the next day. It was known that he was carrying a fairly large sum of money.

Eight days later, his body was fished out of the canal in the presence of Requin, attracted as usual like a crow to carrion. Among the crowd of disreputable characters attracted by the discovery, Requin overheard a murmured remark spoken by an obvious pimp to one of the local tarts. 'Ah! La Cyclope strikes again! If that had been a dame, La Cyclope would have cut her up!' The woman replied, 'No, it's the Hyena; he's just given him a bath in the canal. I know the style.'

Requin with nostrils quivering whistled up the other inspectors of his squad, who were posted around, and took the pimp and the tart into custody. While the corpse was being taken to the morgue, these two characters were hauled off to the examining magistrate to explain what they knew of the fate of the murdered man. Both were at first reticent and maintained that the words they had exchanged had nothing to do with Becker who was unknown to them. But, unfortunately for them, one of the men in the crowd who had been called upon to identify Becker also recognised the pimp as one of the mob of no-goods, who had presumably taken Becker home on the night of the crime.

The pimp, whose name was Louis Marjotte, happened to be an ex-convict. Finding himself in the hands of the police again, he took fright and, to get himself and his girl out of trouble, he denounced the murderers of the American, La Cyclope and her male accomplice, the Hyena.

The Hyena, also known as the Killer of the rue de la Vierge, was the head of a gang, in partnership with La Cyclope, of pimps, layabouts and dockers of the district. La Cylope and the Hyena were not a pretty pair. According to Claude, La Cyclope was a horrible little woman of a most repugnant appearance. Thin, red-headed and with a parchment-like skin, she was pock marked since early youth. As a result of smallpox she had lost one eye, hence her name, the female Cyclops. A hideous scar was all that was left of one eye, while the other had moved over in a strange way, due to convulsions, almost to the centre of her forehead. Claude, always prone to quote the classics at the drop of a hat, says that her hair, parted in two snake-like tresses, recalled the Gorgon's head, the essence of gruesome mythology.

Her spouse, the Hyena, was a worthy partner. A great brute, all arms and legs, with enormous feet. His body carried a most singular head, deathly pale and rising to a point from his hunched shoulders. His lipless face stared out like the head of a vulture, the neck concealed in its feathers; or like the muzzle of a hyena with its head low, ready to fall upon its prey. Claude could really go to town when it came to describing villains. We are really in Frankenstein country here.

These two monsters, who were responsible for at least six recent murders or drownings in the canal at La Villette, lived in the rue de la Vierge near the old Saint-Martin gate of Paris. It was a sinister spot outside the city. It ran into open country and was an ideal rendezvous for rogues and vagabonds. The street, if street it could be called, took its name from a statue of the Virgin and Child set in a niche on the house, an ironic comment on the nature of the inhabitants.

La Cyclope operated at night. Posing as a begger, she would approach anyone passing near the Ourcq canal with a pitiful story of small children to feed. While the late traveller was fumbling in his pocket for a small almsgiving, the gang would attack, rob and kill him after which his body would be thrown into the canal.

Sometimes the gang would wait for pay-day on Saturday, as in the case of Becker the American, and pose as workers in one of the low taverns in the vicinity. The usual method was to get a real worker drunk and then offer to take him or her home. 'Home' usually proved to be the canal. The Hyena, the spouse of La Cyclope, was given to the Saturday night operation. La Cyclope made a speciality of the women victims. Describing her begging technique, Claude says that she conducted them to death on the wings of charity! In fact, three young women had been murdered in one month by La Cyclope. She had her own method, as the Hyena had his, of disposing of the victims. Hers involved disfiguring them with a large pair of scissors before helping the Hyena to throw them into the canal. Hence the remark by the tart to the pimp at the beginning of this story.

The Hyena was an ex-convict, who had already served two sentences for crimes of robbery followed by murder, but in which the murders had not been proved. His method was simpler than that of La Cyclope. A knife-thrust through the heart and then, into the canal. His quick expedition of his victims called forth a remarkable reproach from La Cyclope: 'My husband, my Hyena, my darling, is a no-good! He doesn't know how to make people suffer!' At that time, her devotion to her partner was weakening; she had begun to take a fancy to Louis Marjotte, one of the lieutenants of the gang now safely in the hands of the police and anxious to save his own skin by 'helping them in their enquiries'.

He and Requin between them concocted a plan to cause

109

jealousy in the happy little nest in the house in the rue de la Vierge, where, as Claude says, the two partners were united more by murder than by affection. Briefed by Marjotte, Requin penetrated the lair of the Hyena and La Cyclope by announcing that he was a convict on the run and desirous of joining the gang. 'My prison name is Spanish Liquorice!' One must give the Paris *Sûreté* a prize for nicknames. 'I've come on the recommendation of Marjotte, who has just been pinched in the Becker affair. In fact, things are not looking too bright for you at the moment.' 'Aha!' cried La Cyclope 'So you come to us when you think we're on the spot. Not bad, eh, my love?' This addressed to the Hyena. Then she turned her vitreous eye on Requin. 'If you don't trust me,' said he, 'you're wrong. I'm all right; it's you who should be worried.'

'Listen, my lad.' said La Cyclope, 'I'd like to think this over before we take on an outsider. Let's talk business. Even if I've only got one eye, it's a good one. Before we do anything for you, let's see what there is in it for us. You say you come from Marjotte and that they've just fished out this stiff of a Becker. What then?'

So Requin goes into his act and suggests that Marjotte's 'wife' is jealous of La Cyclope and that she has denounced La Cyclope to the police because she tried to get round Marjotte. 'Though of course I don't believe it,' adds Requin. That any normal woman could be jealous of La Cyclope seems unlikely, but that is Requin's story and his purpose is to rouse the Hyena's jealousy. He broke in, 'If I thought that what Marjotte's doll says is true and that she's doing it to save her skin, I'd send you back damn quick!' But the Hyena did appear to be a bit suspicious of La Cyclope. The seed was sown and he was about to throw a bottle at her. It so happened that they were emptying one when the bogus convict Requin walked in.

La Cyclope was not a little scared of the Hyena. 'Oh, that woman's got a bee in her bonnet. If she has denounced us, as Spanish Liquorice says, so much the worse for her. I'll handle her!' She did not want the Hyena to get jealous, since it was not the first time he had doubted her loyalty.

At this stage another bottle was called for and Requin felt he was getting somewhere. But while La Cyclope was on her way to the cellar, she began to doubt the credentials of Spanish Liquorice. She was strengthened in this conviction when she went upstairs for a moment and looked out of the window. Then she saw Requin's men disposing themselves strategically though in my opinion rather carelessly around the countryside. 'That's it,' she said to herself, 'we're pinched!' She seized a small packet of arsenic. It is just as well to have a packet of arsenic around if you are up to no good. Then she went down to the cellar for another bottle.

While she was away, the idea grew on the Hyena that La Cyclope was transferring her allegiance to Marjotte with a view to making him the head of the gang. So he poured some white powder into her half-filled glass. It was part of the arsenic stock from upstairs. When La Cyclope returned with the bottle, she made a sign to the Hyena that Spanish Liquorice was a cop. Requin had of course seen the white powder go into the glass but had not batted an eyelid. The Hyena had got the message and while he was filling Requin's glass, he allowed La Cyclope to slip the contents of her packet in as well while she was pretending to whisper to the Hyena. So one lot of poison was in La Cyclope's glass and the other in that of Requin. The only safe drink was the Hyena's.

This was the moment of truth and it will be seen that a

policeman's lot is not a happy one. 'Let's drink up!' said the Hyena. Just as Spanish Liquorice was about to raise his glass, he gained a short respite by suggesting that they clink glasses. 'To your health!' said the two villains. Requin had to think fast. He suddenly put his glass down. 'Do you hear that? Something's going on outside. Go see what's happening!' The two monsters rushed to the window while the adroit Requin quickly switched glasses with the Hyena. 'False alarm!' said he, as they returned to the table. 'Let's drink up!'

All this sounds a bit too easy to me but, according to Claude, that is how it happened. Anyway, they drank, Requin happy in the thought that his was the only safe drink. So, as he had planned with Marjotte, he then outlined a scheme for a robbery based on an old adventure in the police records. They fell for it and Requin announced that he would go and get the rest of the gang to work out the details of the project. For their part they seemed to be glad to see him go before the arsenic took effect.

Thus Requin went off to rejoin his waiting inspectors, who by then were either concealed in the grass or hidden behind carts. He told them that all they had to do was to watch and wait. 'You won't have to go into the trap,' he said 'The job's done. You won't even need a scaffold for them!'

By the time the flying squad did break in, there were indeed just two corpses awaiting them and when Requin made his report later to the *Préfecture,* it was of a double suicide in the rue de la Vierge. And that was what appeared in the press at the time.

But that was not the truth. As soon as La Cyclope felt the effect of the poison, she accused the Hyena because of his jealousy of Marjotte. Knowing that what she said was true, he jumped up in a fury and was about to throw the bottle at her when he in his turn realised that he had been poisoned too. He then accused La Cyclope of trying to get rid of him to make Marjotte the head of the gang. Requin had certainly sown the seeds of distrust in this happy household. It appeared later that a fearful struggle had then taken place while they were in their death convulsions. Requin and his men found the two bodies interlocked in a murderous embrace. The Hyena had half a broken bottle in his hand, the rest of the bottle having been pressed into the face of La Cyclope, which could not have done much to improve her already failing charms.

Claude rises to the occasion for the fall of the curtain on the case of the Murders in the rue de la Vierge; 'Both were swimming in a lake of wine and blood!' I offer this tableau to Madame Tussaud's as a *pièce de résistance* in the Chamber of Horrors.

CHAPTER ELEVEN

ZOE, LA BELLE FRISETTE

ALL PIMPS ARE NOT CONVICTS; BUT IT CAN BE STATED WITH CERTAINTY that all convicts are pimps. This is laid down by Monsieur Claude as firmly as any of the theorems of Euclid.

With this pronouncement the story of Zoe, la Belle Frisette, began in January 1872. She was then twenty-seven, a well-known tart who owed her nickname of Frizzy Zoe to her opulent hair which she wore in a fringe across her forehead. She was small with a minute waist and it was said that her cheeky good looks had a special appeal for the local libertines. Though she had a wide choice of *clientèle,* her two favourite pimps could be said to have had their limitations. A pimp in those days was called an Alphonse, and her two Alphonses could well take their places beside the monstrous pair in the previous story. It will be seen that the horror charade of the Paris of 1872 was not confined to the district of La Villette.

Zoe's two protectors, known as Béquillard and Crampon, spent the time during the day as card-sharpers and tricksters. Their victims stood a fair chance of being bashed on the head with Béquillard's crutch or harpooned on the hook which replaced one of Crampon's arms, Béquillard, incidentally, means the one with the crutch and Crampon, hook or grappling iron. The criminal life of the Second Empire was nothing if not picturesque. In this story, however, let us refer henceforth to these two gentlemen as Crutch and Hook.

One day, they were both caught in a police round-up and detained for a while in prison, so Zoe was forced to take on a new defender both to safeguard her person and protect the receipts. Tired of the two cripples and their revolting ways, she went to the other extreme and enlisted a giant, a veritable Apollo in looks. Physically he was very desirable but in disposition he differed little from Crutch and Hook. Still, they

were mere thieves whereas the new favourite was to graduate
to murder. His name was Jean-Baptiste Moreux and he was an
ex-convict.

One Saturday in January 1872, Zoe returned home to the rue
Cambronne accompanied by a man soon after eleven o'clock at
night. She was not seen on the Sunday and her room remained
closed all day. On the Monday the neighbours, alarmed at her
non-appearance, called a locksmith to open her door.

There lay Zoe, la Belle Frisette, on her bed. The local doctor
was called and he pronounced her dead. According to him, she
had died from congestion of the lungs. She was duly buried and
that could have been the end of the story, which would have
been a pity, since Crutch and Hook have so far made but a brief
appearance and still have their parts to play.

If the doctor was satisfied, the neighbours were not. The
drawer of Zoe's dressing table was in disorder and her silk
dress and watch had disappeared. When it was reported that
the silk dress and the watch were being worn by the legitimate
wife of Zoe's temporary husband and protector, it was time to
go to the police.

Enter Monsieur Claude. In a case such as this, he pointed out
that it behoved him and his aides, obscure and indefatigable
servants of the law, to heap Pelion upon Ossa to discover the
truth. It looked like a clear case, but the dress and the watch
had to be verified, the body of course, had already been buried,
and furthermore, any one of her many passing lovers could
have killed her, if it was indeed a case of murder.

It was Zoe's dressmaker, one Elisa, who had recognised the
dress on the new pimp's wife. In 1866, Moreux had married
this young woman but had kept his past a secret. As an ex-
convict he was under police surveillance, but had managed to

stay in Paris without police authorisation by assuming the name of his brother. Under this name he had got a job in a factory. When the wife found out about his police record, she promptly left him and did not see him again until he turned up in 1872 with a gift of a silk dress and watch! He then disappeared. She took the gifts in all innocence and now was prepared to give them up to the police. She was without doubt an honest woman so the trail ended there.

The next discovery was more interesting. Under Zoe's pillow a man's snuffbox was found. Personally I see no purpose in taking a snuffbox to bed with a woman but there it undeniably was. When this object was exhibited round the neighbourhood, it was at once recognised as belonging to Hook, the one-armed pimp. Thus it appeared that it was not Moreux who had spent the night of the alleged crime with Zoe. Could it have been Hook and had he murdered her?

To give the reader some idea of the seething underworld of the Paris in which these events took place, and to fill in the story up to the time Moreux assumed control of Zoe's affairs, let us consider the methods of Crutch and Hook. Among Zoe's many customers had been a licentious old man called G (again the infuriating initial!), whose physical attractions having somewhat declined with the passing years, had to devise a method for stimulating the interest of the local tarts. His technique was to carry a purse full of gold, which he displayed at the opening of negotiations, in the hope of enticing the tart who would think she was onto a good thing. Once his business with her was concluded, however, it was his custom to pay the bare tariff price for such transactions, and the purse of gold remained firmly closed. Zoe had frequently complained to Crutch and Hook of the miserly tricks of this particular client who always employed her with the vague promise of a big pay-off and then did not even add a tip to the bill, so Crutch and Hook determined to get him, and the contents of his purse. With the aid of Zoe, they arranged three consecutive ambushes, but they were unaware that the police were also keeping an eye on the libidinous G. One attempt at the rue Maubuée and another at the Café de Venise failed thanks to the proximity of the police. The third try, outside a dance hall in the Batignolles with Zoe leading G to the slaughter, looked as if it would succeed.

Zoe released the old man's arm as the one-armed man came up and held him fast with his hook. Then Crutch arrived, ready to aim a blow at G while Hook searched for the purse. G let out a cry for help and at that moment the police appeared and grabbed both Crutch and Hook. La Belle Frisette at once disowned her gallant protectors. Though she got away with it, the police thereafter kept a watch on her. With Crutch and Hook under lock and key for a while, she had preforce to seek the protection of Moreux.

But was Zoe really attached to Moreux? Claude thought that she was still fond of Hook. And as soon as Hook was released, whose snuffbox was found under her pillow? Hook's. Perhaps Hook's jealousy was the motive for the crime, or perhaps Hook and Moreux together murdered her. However, Crutch said that they could not stand one another, so they were hardly likely to work in concert. In the meantime Zoe's body was exhumed and the real cause of death ascertained, strangulation.

The events of the evening before the murder had now to be investigated. Zoe had been drinking with a German in a café. He was located and he said that Zoe had told him a tale. It is curious that whores usually try to give themselves some kind of human identity, with a story of a child in the country, an unhappy family life, an estranged or cruel husband, or a vague connection with a higher stratum of society. An attempt, perhaps, to elicit a degree of sympathy and avoid being treated as a mere object or simply to obtain a more generous fee. Anyway, Zoe told the German a hard luck story about how she disliked Moreux who in any event was married. What she needed was a protector like the German, since she knew that Moreux would eventually abandon her and return to his real wife. But the German was too wary and Zoe left him and returned alone to her room. The German afterwards saw a man apparently awaiting her at her door, though he could not say if it was Moreux or Hook.

Hook, by now in custody again, was shown the snuffbox. He denied that it was his and said it had been given as a present by Zoe to Moreux. 'Let me see him,' he said. 'you'll soon see that it's not I who screwed Zoe's neck. Why the hell should I kill the goose that laid the golden eggs?' Hook's obvious jealousy of Moreux put Claude on the trail at last. He confronted Hook with Moreux in the office of the *juge d'instruction.* As both denied murdering Zoe, the snuffbox was produced. Moreux had clearly forgotten this fatal slip in leaving his snuffbox at the scene of the crime. He detested Hook as much as Hook hated him, and was furious at Hook's allegation that the snuffbox belonged to him, Moreux. 'He stole it from me!' he shouted, 'because Zoe had given it to me. She gave it to me several days before she died. *And* she gave me the dress and watch too!'

The the *juge d'instruction* intervened. 'Let us suppose,' he said, 'that, instead of being given to you by Zoe or stolen by Hook, it had simply been forgotten by you and left in her bed.'

At this, Moreux broke down and admitted that he had done it. The sight of the hated Hook seemed to enrage him and all his loathing of Hook came out. 'It wasn't for the three hundred francs in her drawer, it wasn't for the silk dress and the watch I stole that I strangled her. No, it was because I was sick of Hook. She was always talking about Hook. Even in my arms she was still talking about Hook. It's *him* not Zoe who has brought me to this!'

Hook was released though the police continued to watch him. Later, in the prison of La Roquette, Claude asked Moreux why he had dumped the incriminating evidence of the dress and watch on his wife. 'I wanted to compromise her,' he replied. 'She got on my nerves with her mealymouthed ways just as much as Zoe did with her passion for Hook. Anyway, I didn't get anywhere with that any more than I did with Zoe. If Zoe had played fair with me, she'd still be alive. Charlot can start sharpening up his knife!' Charlot was the popular name for the public executioner.

According to Claude, Zoe had taken on Moreux for his strength as a protector as well as for the fact that he was rather dim-witted. She roused his jealousy over Hook who, though deformed, was far more intelligent. Indeed she hoped that Hook would come back to her when he was released from prison, as she knew that he had a scheme or two which might benefit her up his one sleeve. It was without doubt his inferiority complex which drove Moreux to murder her. Zoe more or less got what was coming to her.

Moreux with a criminal record since the age of fifteen could not expect leniency. The *crime passionnel* is not usually admitted among the lower orders, though it is argued more successfully in the upper ranks of society, so Moreux was sentenced to death by the guillotine.

In June 1872 he was executed. There was a new executioner for the occasion, and Moreux was his first customer. He approached the guillotine with resignation, looked at it and remarked, 'So that's all it is!' He pressed the spring and Moreux died. One of the executioner's assistants looked with admiration at his new boss and commented, 'Not bad for a beginner!'

The romantic Claude sees a parallel between Moreux and Zoe and the story of des Grieux and Manon Lescaut. However, as spectators a century later, we probably cannot help feeling that the world was not much poorer for the passing of both Zoe, la Belle Frisette, and the pimp Moreux. I myself rather regret that Messrs Crutch and Hook could not have gone too.

CHAPTER TWELVE

THE FOUR HORSEMEN AND THE LYONS MAIL

THERE ARE MANY ROGUES IN THE *DRAMATIS PERSONAE* OF THIS STORY, which has remained a mystery from the end of the eighteenth century to the present day. We still cannot be sure who the real rogues were. What would your judgment have been *at that time?*

Let us assume that you come from Godalming. You are in London for the day. Walking over Westminster Bridge you run into a friend, one of your neighbours. He says, 'Hallo, fancy meeting you here! What are you doing?' You say you are spending a leisurely day in town and ask him what he is doing. Your neighbour explains that he has got mixed up quite innocently in some business with the police and has to give some information about a recent murder case. He is now on his way to Scotland Yard to recover some of his papers which the police wanted to look at. It is just a formality. It won't take long. Would you care to walk as far as the Yard with him? You've nothing else to do so you stroll over the bridge together. You get to the Yard and, as you go in, two women in the waiting room seem very agitated. They go to the policeman at the door and whisper something to him. Your friend's name is called and he asks you to go in with him. He collects his papers and you are about to leave when the inspector says, 'Just a minute, please!' to *you*. The door closes behind you and he then tells you that you have been positively identified by two important women witnesses as one of those concerned in the recent murder. You are arrested there and then and eventually put on trial. All your alibis are swept aside in the face of the sworn testimony of these women. You are sentenced to death. Appeals to mercy, reason, common-sense, justice and humanity are ignored. You write a farewell letter to your wife and children protesting your innocence and you go to your doom.

This is a mad dream, of course, and this is the point at which you wake up screaming. But no, it is not. It is the nightmare which, *mutatis mutandis,* Joseph Lesurques lived – and died – in Paris in 1796.

By many believed to be one of the greatest judicial errors of all time, the story of the Lyons Mail has been told again and again. Until quite late into the nineteenth century the descendants of Lesurques sought to have the case re-opened but his name was never cleared. Was Lesurques guilty or was he the victim of a frightful error? The element of mystery remains, but you can judge for yourself.

Towards the end of the eighteenth century, the mail from Paris to Lyons was carried in a two-wheeled wagon drawn by three horses, one of which was ridden by a postilion. The wagon was covered by a heavy canvas hood and was accessible from the front and back. On the evening of the 27th April 1796 or, as it was then called in the revolutionary calendar, 8th *Floréal,* it had been waiting in Paris for several hours for the mail from Brest. Finally, it set off, rather late, from the rue Martin, carrying mail and a very large quantity of paper money for the army in Italy. Curiously enough there was no escort for such a valuable load, except for the postilion and a post office employee. There were one or two benches for passengers in the wagon, which could not have offered much comfort on the roads of those days. That evening there was one solitary traveller. He was dressed in a brown overcoat below which the end of a sabre could be seen. We shall hear of him again.

Next morning some peasants going early to work between Lieusaint and Melun found the mail wagon abandoned at a place called La Closeaux. The dead bodies of the postilion and the post office courier lay close by covered with blood. The postilion had been horribly mutilated. Two of the three horses had been hitched to a tree. There was no sign of the passenger but a broken sabre and a silver-plated spur were found on the spot. Of the contents of the wagon there was no sign.

The officers of the law were soon on their way from Melun. It was clear that the postilion had put up a fight for his life; his skull was split, he had three large wounds in the chest and one hand had been almost hacked off. The other man had been stabbed several times in the neck and in the body. *Rigor mortis* has set in, indicating that the crime had been committed the night before or in the very early hours of the morning.

Enquiries were made all round the district. One man had seen four horsemen the previous evening going towards Lieusaint from Melun. Later, on his return, he had seen one of the men galloping while the other three trotted nearby. The proprietress of an inn at Lieusaint had served four men. One of them had come back to retrieve his sabre which he had left behind. One had borrowed a piece of string to attach his broken spur! Another innkeeper had served them with dinner and was able to give a description. Several other locals testified to having seen the four horsemen. Two witnesses, who were to play a dramatic part in the case, were women servants from Montgeron, a point between Lieusaint and Paris. In fact the four horsemen seem to have been remarkably careless in allowing themselves to be seen by so many people near the scene of the crime.

The obvious question was, who was the mysterious passenger with the sabre? We shall not know yet. Other evidence and witnesses continued to accumulate. A guard at the Rambouillet gate of Paris had seen five horsemen early that morning arrive from the direction of Melun, their horses obviously tired out.

Then a single horse was found wandering loose in Paris and was recognised as the third one from the team drawing the mail. It was also found that a man had brought four horses at five o'clock that morning to an inn kept by a man named Aubry. They were taken away again at seven by the same man, whose name was believed to be Etienne. He was accompanied by one Bernard. Etienne's surname was found to be Couriol. When further enquiries were made, it was learned that he had slept out on the night of the crime, but had since disappeared. Normally he slept with his mistress at a house kept by a man named Richard. Richard and his wife were arrested and they gave the information that Couriol had left for Château-Thierry.

Thus the principal suspects so far were the unknown passenger with the sabre, Couriol and Bernard. Nothing was known of the first, except that he had paid his fare and had no baggage. He had dined with the courier before the mail left.

The first step was to get hold of Couriol, who was found at Château-Thierry at the house of a man called Gohier. Here the police found a bag containing part of the paper money missing from the Lyons Mail. Couriol and his mistress were arrested and lodged in prison in Paris. Also found at the Gohier house was a man known as Guénot. He apparently knew nothing but the police seized his papers and told him that he would be required for questioning in Paris, after which he would get his papers back.

A few days later he was in Paris crossing the Pont-Neuf to retrieve his papers as instructed. Now Guénot was a native of Douai and on the bridge he met an old neighbour of his, one Joseph Lesurques. It so happened that the Richards, at whose house Couriol used to sleep, were also natives of Douai and in fact Guénot had introduced the Richards to Lesurques, who had had dinner with them a few days before the crime in company with Gohier, Guénot, Couriol and Couriol's mistress. On the bridge Guénot told Lesurques about his little bother with the police at Château-Thierry and suggested that they walk to the *Palais de Justice* together to get his papers.

In the waiting room were two women, who appeared to be very excited when they saw the two men enter. The women went in first. They were the two servants from Montgeron. They told the *juge d'instruction* that on the afternoon of 8th *Floréal*, which you will remember was the date on which the Lyons Mail stood waiting for the mail from Brest, they saw four men at Montgeron. One of the women deposed that the four had eaten at the inn where she worked and had taken coffee at the house of a woman called Chatelain, leaving afterwards in the direction of Lieusaint. Both women recognised the two men in the waiting room as two of the men in question. Guénot was then called in and detained for questioning. The police also detained Lesurques and searched him. They found two identity cards, one in the name of a relative, André Lesurques, and the other blank! Thus began what was to be called the martyrdom of Joseph Lesurques.

At this stage, one point which does not seem to have been raised in this case may be mentioned. If Lesurques were guilty, why did he go and put his head in the lion's mouth? Surely a man with blood on his hands would have kept waay from the *Palais de Justice.* It might have been a point in his favour that he *did* go there that day or on the other hand he might have gone out of bravado. Some criminals are made that way. Still, one cannot help feeling that it was the act of an innocent man.

The general round-up finally produced six accused; Couriol, Guénot, Richard, Bernard, Lesurques and one Bruer, who had been arrested at the same time as Richard. Of these, Bruer and Guénot were freed. Guénot had an excellent alibi, though he had been identified by the two servants from Montgeron. Richard was condemned to penal servitude for twenty-four years. Couriol, Bernard and Lesurques were found guilty and executed. At the trial Couriol stated 'that Lesurques did not take part in the crime.' On the way from the prison to the scaffold, he shouted repeatedly, 'I am guilty. Lesurques is innocent!' According to Couriol, the other four guilty men were Dubosq, a well-known criminal, Vidal, an associate of Dubosq from Lyons, Roussi, an Italian, and Durochat, the man with the sabre.

Durochat was found to be in prison on a charge of theft. He was recognised by a post office official who saw him get into the Lyons mail wagon, as the man with the sabre. Durochat admitted his guilt and confirmed Couriol's account of the crime, naming the same men. Durochat said that he had never known Lesurques.

Vidal and Dubosq were arrested and confronted with Durochat, who recognised Vidal but was not sure about Dubosq. Durochat was executed. Dubosq escaped from custody after the confrontation with Durochat and was not recaptured till December 1800. Vidal was tried alone, found guilty and executed. Thus five so far had been guillotined for the crime.

When Dubosq was eventually caught, Richard was brought from prison as a witness. He told of a quarrel between Durochat, Roussi, Vidal and Dubosq at Couriol's, where they were disputing a share out of loot. He said that Couriol had told him that he (Couriol) and Dubosq had murdered the postilion. Roussi was not located until 1803. He was extradited from Madrid, tried, found guilty, and executed. Roussi said at his trial that Lesurques was innocent. By then, seven people in all, including Lesurques had been executed for this crime.

It is clear that six of these were guilty in some measure or other. However, it is with Lesurques that we are concerned here. Before going into the details of his defence, we must anticipate and deal with the trial of Dubosq more than three years later. It was then becoming obvious that here was a case of mistaken identity. Lesurques had the misfortune to resemble Dubosq. At the trial of the latter, several of the witnesses from the first trial did not recognise Dubosq and they confirmed their identification of Lesurques. Partisans of Lesurques had hoped that the trial and conviction of Dubosq would exonerate Lesurques, but witnesses persisted in their evidence and one recalled that he had been able to identify Lesurques because he was the man who had asked for a piece of string to tie his spur. And you will remember the broken spur found at the scene of the crime. Dubosq was even given a wig, made of hair of the same colour as a lock given by Lesurques to his wife. The witnesses were called again and all confirmed their former depositions, except ome woman from Lieusaint, who announced dramatically, 'At the trial of Lesurques, I identified him but my conscience now tells me that I was mistaken. I know now that it was not Lesurques I saw but Dubosq, that man there!' Sensation in court, but unfortunately Dubosq's condemnation could not clear Lesurques, because they were not charged with the same offence. Dubosq was charged with assisting in the crime and not of actually committing the murders. He was nevertheless executed.

Let us now look at the case against Lesurques. He came of quite respectable people. He had done his military service after leaving college at the age of eighteen. He later married and had three children. By speculation he had made quite a sum of money, from which he enjoyed an income. However, he had come to find life in Douai rather dull and had gone to Paris the year before the crime, leaving his family behind. He lived with his cousin, André, whose indentity card, you recall, was found on him when he was arrested. He had made the acquaintance of a young woman, Eugénie Dargence, and he lived with her occasionally. He was a lazy, careless young man. In all the time he was in Paris, he had not taken the trouble to get himself an identity card, which was very necessary in those days. The two cards found on him brought him under suspicion at once. Asked about the blank one, he said it had been given to him by a man whose name he had forgotten. How often do we find in the criminal records the old story, 'I bought it from a man in a pub!' The police said that he had been living beyond his means and that he was in need of funds for some of his financial transactions at the beginning of 1796. Thus a slender motive was introduced.

His first alibi broke down disastrously. A jeweller gave evidence that Lesurques was in Paris at his office for several hours when he was alleged to have been in the vicinity of Montgeron. He had bought some earrings and had sold a spoon. How could this be proved? The jeweller could produce his book in which the transactions were recorded on the fatal date. The book was produced and the date had clearly been altered! Lesurques however produced other quite convincing alibis from people who had seen him and spent time with him on both 8th and 9th *Floréal*. But the altered date, which was never properly explained, though the witness was arrested for perjury, left a very bad impression. Then his mistress gave evidence that he had visited her on the evening of the 8th. An unlettered working girl, she had to admit under cross-examination that she was not familiar with the revolutionary calendar and could not give the name of the month preceding *Floréal.* Her evidence did not help at all.

Lesurques protested his innocence. Couriol, on trial with him, confirmed that he had no part in the affair. Though the judge was uneasy about Couriol's affirmation of the innocence of Lesurques, it could not weigh against the evidence of the two women and others, and the faulty alibis. The judge was still uneasy when he confronted Durochat with Vidal and Dubosq. If Durochat had been able to recognise Dubosq with certainty, it would have been in favour of Lesurques, even though he had been executed by then. It must also be remembered that Lesurques did not choose his company very carefully. He was known to be associated with Couriol and the Richards. This is not evidence that he committed any crime but it does not help in conjunction with the other evidence against him. While one may point to the statements of Durochat and Couriol, is it not strange that Dubosq made no reference to Lesurques? It might be argued that he could have exonerated Lesurques, if not at his own trial at least at the foot of the scaffold when he knew that all was lost. But he said nothing.

It has been shown again and again that positive indentification can be a very tricky business. The case of Adolf Beck is a classic example. If you were asked many weeks later, to identify a man whom you saw talking to a little girl on a bus one day, how sure could you be? You would have no reason for taking any particular notice at the time. In the case of Lesurques we have a number of illiterate peasants who were giving evidence at the trial of Dubosq three years later. How sure could they be?

Over a period of sixty years the family of Lesurques sought

to have his innocence established. The judge, who had been prejudiced against him at the trial, although taking into account the statement of Couriol, addressed a memorandum to the Emperor Napoleon in 1806, urging the rehabilitation of Lesurques. The Emperor received Lesurques' children but dismissed a plea for a re-trial. His widow, still faithful to him despite his infidelity to her, applied to the Chamber of Deputies in 1821. The Procurator of Versailles was called upon for a report and he concluded that Lesurques was innocent, but this was not enough. A further and more detailed report was ordered and the finding was reversed. The widow died in 1842 exhausted after years of striving with the courts. Then in 1845 his daughter drowned herself in the Seine after yet another attempt to clear her father. Her son took up the struggle. One examination of the case which was ordered came to nothing on account of a *coup d'état.* He tried again and again, even appealing to the Empress Eugénie, who was favourably impressed, but this too failed. He died comparatively young of mortification and despair. Other relatives continued to work for a revision of the case. The last applications were made in 1868 and were duly turned down. The last grand-daughter lost her three children in tragic circumstances and herself died in the war of 1870, so the family of Lesurques died out, pursued by the Furies since that encounter on the Pont-Neuf in 1796.

In 1868, the authorities were still not convinced that Lesurques had been mistaken for Dubosq and saw no reason why they could not have both been present on the fatal night.

There the matter rests. It is as well to remember that some of the evidence in favour of Lesurques was produced after his trial and execution. For those concerned with the trial and condemnation, there was the evidence of the eye-witnesses, there were the threadbare alibis, his acknowledged association with people known to have had a hand in the murder and robbery, his need of money and his general mode of life. Moreover Dubosq was not tried till more than three years later. What would your judgment have been? It is clear that Dubosq was there near Lieusaint on the night of 8th/9th *Floréal*. Was Lesurques there too?

CHAPTER THIRTEEN

SATISFIED CUSTOMER

Cyrus J had just finished haranguing the European sales Convention of the firm of Cyrus J Schmolz & Company, of which he, as Cyrus J Schmolz III, was President. The original Cyrus J Schmolz had given Schmolz's Krunching Krackles to a grateful world, and since the demise of that pious humbug, a large percentage of the human race, save a few head-hunters in New Guinea and a handful of Eskimos in the remote Arctic regions, had daily breakfasted on that nourishing cereal. As a result Cyrus J Schmolz II had become a millionaire. The third of that dynasty, with whom we are here concerned, had so much money and so little time, after bullying his thousands of employees all over the globe, that he had never been able to count it.

Cyrus J III was the greatest salesman in the world. He said so. He could sell anything and anybody. No wooden nickels for him! Having roared himself hoarse at the Convention with such original phrases as 'Get on or get out!' and 'Never leave a prospect until he's a satisfied customer!' he fired a few of the faithful employees, hired a few others to replace them, packed his Roget's *Thesaurus,* where he found the incredible words with which he larded his speeches, and left for Florence for a few days of relaxation.

There, in search of culture and something on which to spend the dollars wrung from the sales of Schmolz's Krunching Krackles, he became acquainted with a noble family which had fallen upon hard times. Cyrus J relaxed in the fifteenth century *palazzo.* My, what would the folks say back in Milwaukee! There on the walls were the arms of the Medici. That dagger had been worn by Lorenzo the Magnificent. All round the room were portraits of generations of the noble house, the head of which sat opposite him in a chair which had once belonged to

Pope Alexander VI. Grand Dukes and their voluptuous courtesans had feasted at that table.

'Say, how do you go about getting a room together like this?' he asked the Count. 'Sir,' said that aged aristocrat, 'you begin five, six, seven centuries ago!' The answer ricochetted from Cyrus J like a .22 from a rhino's hide. Then Cyrus J was told the sad story of the decline of the noble house from fabulous riches in the quattrocento to postwar Italy and the almost worthless lira; of the need to consider selling the most precious possessions held in trust from a long line of noble ancestors. The very things among which they sat would have to go. Still, the Count was the last of his line and what did it matter in an atomic world?

'Why, Count, do you mean you're selling up?' The old Count nodded sadly and the Countess, who had just come in, brushed away *una furtiva lagrima.* Even Cyrus J was moved. 'It all goes to the auctioneer next week,' said the Count, 'and in these days it will go for a song.' Cyrus J's heart beat a little faster. He could visualise that room in the red sandstone monstrosity he had built himself in Milwaukee. Yes, Sir, he would do the old Count a good turn, and enhance his own prestige back home. Slowly the old man exhibited and described his treasures one by one. Finally Cyrus J could contain himself no longer. He offered to buy the room as it stood.

The aged Count was reluctant, a pitiful relic of the fifteenth century. His eyes filled with tears. He spoke with dignity, the dignity of princely forebears, of a family which had given the world three popes. 'My friend,' he said, 'for I hope I may call you my friend, to part with this room is to cut off my right arm, but I would prefer you to have it rather than sell it in the public market place.' He would not mention a figure. A descendant of the princes of the Renaissance does not mention figures. Cyrus J had no such embarrassment. He mentioned a figure, large in dollars, but astronomic in lire. It sounded like the distance to one of the planets. 'Then take it with my blessing!' said the Count and the deal was sealed with a bottle of a fine vintage from the Count's own cellar and a cheque on the National City Bank of New York.

Next day, the treasures were removed for crating. The old Count could not bear to be present to see their passing. The paintings, the statuary, the lovely old furniture, the chair of the Borgia pope, the Medici dagger, the bronzes; all were packed up for the forwarding agents and now the room was bare. An old family retainer was mournfully sweeping up.

The old Count walked in. The faithful servant looked up, his eyes full of sympathy. 'Well, Luigi,' said his master, 'thank God we've got rid of that junk! Move the real stuff back as soon as you can.'

CHAPTER FOURTEEN

STRANGER THAN FICTION

LET US NOW RETURN TO THE ARCHIVES OF THE FRENCH POLICE, IN WHICH we find a story which is already familiar to most of us though in another guise.

A young man is about to be married to a very pretty girl with a handsome dowry. On the eve of the wedding, he is falsely denounced by a rival and unjustly imprisoned. He spends many years cut off from news of the outside world. In captivity he comes to know an old *abbé* who educates him and finally leaves him a vast fortune. The young man eventually regains his liberty, and the rest of the story is about his slow and carefully calculated revenge on the author of his misfortune. Yes, you have heard this before. It is the story of *The Count of Monte Cristo*. It has all the ingredients: thwarted love, misery and torture in a dungeon, immense riches and the power which goes with them and vengeance pursued to the utmost limit.

In France in the first quarter of the nineteenth century, one had to be politically agile to keep out of trouble. The French Revolution had run its course. There were many contenders for power; the men of the Convention, of the Directory and of the Consulate plotted, manoeuvred and murdered, while the *émigrés* schemed for a return of the Bourbons. Probably the most agile of all and without doubt one of the greatest rogues of all time was Joseph Fouché, who in the tradition of the Vicar of Bray survived the Revolution and its aftermath, the Empire, the fall of Napoleon, the Hundred Days and the Restoration of the Bourbons, holding office to the end. It is against this background that this story of vengeance is told.

The young man about to be married was one François Picaud, a cobbler living in Paris in 1807. His *fiancée* was twenty years old, blonde and beautiful, named Marguerite.

140

Picaud was a good-looking young man but poor, while his future bride was to bring a rich dowry to the match. But in this drama the villain is already waiting in the wings. A café proprietor, one Loupian, also had designs on this rich prize. He was a widower with two children and he was not going to let the young Picaud stand in his way. Loupian was a man of action. He went to the Imperial police – for this was in Napoleon's time – and accused Picaud of plotting for the restoration of the Bourbons. Napoleon had been Emperor for little more than two years and his shaky dynasty was hardly established. The police acted quickly in cases like this and did not bother much about the formalities of a trial. Picaud was arrested and disappeared without trace.

Eight years later, the Battle of Waterloo changed the face of Europe. Napoleon himself was in captivity now. In fact, among those who accompanied him as far as England was his faithful Chief of Police, Savary, Duke of Rovigo. About this time, there arrived in Paris a certain Joseph Lucher, who had just been released from prison. While there, he had met and won the friendship of a fellow prisoner, an old Italian priest. He too had been condemned for political reasons. When he died, in 1814, he made Lucher his sole heir to a vast fortune in property, jewels and gold.

On arrival in Paris, Lucher made his way to the quarter formerly inhabited by the luckless Picaud. He made enquiries about him and was told that Picaud had been arrested eight years before, on the accusation of one Loupian – just as he was about to be married. Picaud had disappeared and Loupian had eventually married the girl. Lucher explained that he had known Picaud in prison and that he had interested himself in his case. Of course Lucher was none other than Picaud himself, and Picaud was rich, fabulously rich, with the fortune of the old priest who had shared his imprisonment. He had known that he had been arrested as a Legitimist but now he knew who had denounced him so unjustly, for the charge that he was plotting for the Bourbons was unfounded. However it was the return of Louis XVIII which had secured his release. Now he knew who had robbed him of his bride and condemned him to the long years of agony in a stone cell.

And how had life treated Loupian in the meantime? He was now prosperous, owner of a very large café, and blessed with two children by his second marriage. Long years in prison had taught Lucher to be patient. He did not rush round to Loupian's café with a knife, but quietly continued his enquiries, at times disguised as an *abbé*. His investigations took him to other parts of France to contact old acquaintances who had moved away. He reconstructed the whole story, and paid well for his information. Thus it was that he discovered that one Chaubard and one Solari had aided Loupian in denouncing him in 1807. Chaubard and Solari were still in Paris, and indeed went regularly to Loupian's splendid café.

Picaud, whose appearance had been greatly changed by his long imprisonment, managed to obtain a humble position in Loupian's café, where he worked unrecognised by any of his former associates.

One evening, Chaubard did not turn up for a rendezvous at the café with Solari. He had the best of excuses, as his body was later found with a knife stuck firmly in the heart. On the knife was an inscription, Number One!

You will recall that Loupian had two children by his first marriage. One was a beautiful girl of sixteen, who was being diligently courted by an Italian prince about this time. In fact, the courtship was so assiduous that the marriage was speeded up to anticipate a happy family event. At the wedding feast, from which the prince was unaccountably absent, the news was received that he was no prince but an escaped convict, by then well on his way across the frontier! Such occasions call for a holiday in the country and the sorrowful parents took the daughter away to avoid publicity. In their absence, the café was burnt to the ground and looted. A curious feature of this occurrence was that fires had been lighted at several different points.

The other child of Loupian's first marriage was a boy, who was induced about this time by some drunken comrades to raid a liquor shop. In the course of the escapade they persuaded him to take some silver and jewellery, out of bravado. Strangely enough, someone had tipped off the police and the young man was caught in possession of the proceeds. One may steal liquor but silver and jewellery are another matter. He was sentenced to twenty years' penal servitude. They stood for no nonsense in those days, and penal servitude was penal servitude; there were no TV sets in the cells!

Solari continued to visit his friend Loupian in the more modest café, which the latter had opened after the destruction of the larger establishment. One evening he was poisoned there, and died in horrible agony a few hours later. Picaud, it may be mentioned, was still faithfully serving Loupian despite his master's fallen fortunes. Before Solari was buried, a note was found attached to the funeral draperies bearing the words, Number Two!

In 1820, the beautiful but faithless Marguerite went mad and died. The wretched Loupian by that time must have realised that his own death could not be far off. Indeed, shortly afterwards, he was walking in Paris when a masked man came up to him and said, 'I am Picaud, whom you put in prison. I am Picaud whose bride you stole. It was I who stabbed Chaubard, who poisoned Solari, who dishonoured your daughter, who ruined your son, who burned your house down and caused your wife to die in misery. Now it is your turn. You are Number Three!'

But here everything goes wrong with the story. Just as he cut Loupian's throat, he himself was seized, half strangled and carried off unconscious. He awoke later in a cellar. By his side stood one Allut, an old acquaintance of his Paris days, whom he had sought out at Nîmes when he first came out of prison, and whom he had rewarded for information with a large diamond. That diamond had set Allut on a path of crime and prison. On his release, he had traced Picaud to Paris, bent on revenge and knowing that there were many more diamonds where the original one came from. Allut had followed Picaud step by step and was the only other person who could explain the mysterious deaths of Chaubard and the others to the Paris police.

Allut was armed. He offered to free Picaud and guaranteed his own silence on receipt of exactly one half of the old priest's fortune. Arguments led to quarrels and at the end of a week Allut killed Picaud in a violent struggle. Allut hastily buried the body in the cellar and fled to England. He was already wanted by the police. Picaud's body was not discovered for six years, by which time it was unrecognisable. There the long series of mysteries could have remained unsolved.

But in 1828, Allut lay on his deathbed. Just before he died, he caused a French priest to be summoned, and to him he confided the whole story of Picaud's vengeance and his own part in the story. He asked the priest to communicate the facts to the Paris police. So the dossier was complete in those archives, from which Peuchet, a precursor of Monsieur Claude, gathered material for his *Police Dévoilée* when he retired from the *Préfecture*. And it is possible that Alexandre Dumas in his turn gathered the material for *The Count of Monte Cristo* from that same story. Thus, in the immortal romance, we see the wretched figure of François Picaud behind the more heroic character of Edmond Dantes.

CHAPTER FIFTEEN

THE LOST CORSET:
A KEYSTONE COPS COMEDY

PARIS 1867, WAS THE YEAR OF THE SECOND EXPOSITION UNIVERSELLE. AN exhibition of this kind brings together the achievements of every country in the world with a display of their arts and manufactures in search of new markets. It also attracts rogues and vagabonds, tarts and pickpockets, for here they will most certainly find the gullible and reap a rich harvest. Thus we find Monsieur Claude one day strolling round the galleries and examining, among other items of interest, the great Krupp cannon in the German section. Only three years later Krupp guns were to bring France to defeat in the way of 1870. Having had considerable experience of German espionage, Claude did not share the amusement of his fellow Parisians at this giant weapon. He was full of forebodings and, as he would have phrased it, a prey to sombre thoughts.

This melancholy state of mind must have put Claude off his guard — for in general he was no fool — when he was accosted by a tall man with a ginger beard, broad shoulders and long legs. He at once identified the stranger as an Englishman, though the description hardly fits the traditional image of John Bull. The man introduced himself as the Chief of the English Police, which astonishing statement he confirmed by a card showing his name and qualification. The name was Clarscovich which, even allowing for Claude's lack of knowledge of the English language, would hardly strike one as a fine old English cognomen. He was there, he said, to arrest the numerous pickpockets who infested the exhibition halls. In this function he solicited the co-operation of Monsieur Claude.

Claude seems to have swallowed the unlikely story, though he was intrigued to know how this English colleague had recognised him. He handed back the impressive card and said he would be glad to be of assistance but he would like to know how Mr Clarscovich had been able to identify him. 'Quite easily,' he replied. 'In London, at Scotland Yard, we not only have photographs of all the known criminals but of all the celebrated Chiefs of Police. Yours, Monsieur, is particularly well known to us.' Claude, like the crow in La Fontaine's fable, flattered and beside himself with joy, expresses his willingness to help; and with the same dire results, for you may be sure that from this moment onwards Monsieur Claude is being taken for a ride.

'All I want,' said the Englishman, 'is an exchange of services. If you care to point out to me your bandits who are robbing our visitors to the exhibition, I in my turn will identify our rogues who are out to prey on your visitors!' Monsieur Claude at this stage is simple enough to look upon the encounter as providential. I would have thought that the dimmest constable in *Z Cars* would have telegraphed for confirmation of such a mission, but Claude had no misgivings.

The Paris police at this time had received numerous complaints from visitors to the exhibition of the activities of pickpockets. Among many cases one French visitor had been deprived, according to Claude, by a cross-Channel bandit, helped by a very beautiful Englishwoman, of his wallet containing ten thousand francs. I seldom carry more than ten pounds at a time in any pocket, so I would like to know who these people are who go about with great wads of banknotes in their wallets? Who are these women one reads about who have handbags, crammed with fifty thousand pounds worth of jewellery, stolen? I can only be thankful I am not in the insurance business.

It was this theft of ten thousand francs which had brought Monsieur Claude to the exhibition. It appears that a provincial had come to Paris and had put up at one of the *tavernes anglaises* erected for the occasion. Having been captivated by the sirens employed there, he had been led, after the closing hour of the exhibition, to an orgy, in the course of which he had been robbed of his ten thousand francs. And here was Monsieur Claude on the track of the lost wallet, having lingered in the German section, on his way to the British exhibits.

As one colleague to another, Claude told the *soi-disant* English Chief of Police what had brought him there. What could be easier than that the English colleague should conduct him to the self-same *taverne* where the theft had been planned? 'Come with me,' said the Englishman. 'I think I've got the thief. She's a pretty girl called Miss Palmer, with hair as gold as the money she so efficiently extracts from the customers' pockets.' Policemen rarely, if ever, talk like this but we must take Monsieur Claude's word for it. He offered to be the host, but the Englishman insisted on footing the bill, seeing that the *taverne* was, so to speak, English territory! A nice touch this. With French courtesy, Claude did not insist and the two Chiefs of Police proceeded to the *Café des Anglais*.

The Exhibition of 1867, apart from the displays, consisted of a series of cafés and restaurants representing all countries of the world. From the dusky beauties of the Moorish establishments to the blonde daughters of Albion in their *tavernes*. one had a most ravishing selection. In fact, the Sultan Abdul-Azis was said to have recruited quite a few additions to his harem from this array of beauty. Claude's report is quite lyrical.

Installed at their table, the Englishman pointed out, among half a dozen girls serving champagne at the counter, the most attractive one of the lot. 'There's your Miss Palmer,' said Clarscovich. 'She's the one I suspect of relieving your countryman of ten thousand francs. When they're less busy, I'll call her over.'

After a sumptuous meal, finished off with champagne, the English colleague summoned the girl who came over and joined them. She was apparently all that a French connoisseur of women could wish for. Claude was in a state of ecstasy and he listened with incredible naïvety to her story. Born in Whitechapel of parents who kept the 'Prince Regent' pub, she had graduated through the usual seduction at fifteen and a stretch in prison to leaving home and arriving as a counter girl in this English pub at the exhibition. She made up to Claude who, although he says he did not believe any part of her story, fell for her like a schoolboy. When her usual whore's tale had finished, she finished her glass of champagne in one go and said she did not feel well. Complaining of the heat, she asked the chivalrous Claude to open the window near where they were seated. Then, recovering rapidly, she thanked them both and withdrew.

Just at that moment, another man came up to the Englishman and whispered in his ear in a most agitated way. Clarscovich rose, shook hands with Claude and announced that a very important matter, which his detective had just told him about, required his immediate attention. 'Be sure,' he said. 'this Miss Palmer is a pickpocket and has always been one. She is only at the counter to signal to her lover the pigeons to be plucked. She probably robbed your Frenchman. Now I'm off on another case of theft. You'll be hearing about it and you can share the credit with me. See you tomorrow!' With no further explanation he moved off. Then Claude noticed that the English girl left with him.

This did not seem to worry Claude at the time but he

certainly did not like the look of his English colleague's detective. However, after leaving the *taverne,* Claude went to make a purchase at a stall. He reached into his pocket for the money and found that he had been robbed of his wallet containing a considerable sum. Then he recalled how the girl had leaned against him when he was opening the window for her. No fool like an old fool!

Overcome with shame and rage, Claude summoned one of his inspectors, gave him an exact description of the false detective who had talked to the false Chief of Scotland Yard, instructed him to put every policeman on the trail and find the man by the evening.

At dinner that night, in a café near the Châtelet, one of Claude's men arrived to announce that they had got their man. 'Has he confessed?' asked Claude. The man had come clean. He was a known criminal. Claude realised that he had been completely fooled and robbed into the bargain. From what the man said the two accomplices, the English Chief of Police and Miss Palmer, had been on the game for some time and had acquired something in the region of three hundred thousand francs. They had of course disappeared. Claude wondered if he had been robbed not only for the money but as a joke on the French police. So a few months went by, in which Claude tried to forget how easily he had been taken in.

Then one day, a most elegant character known as the Count de Montgommery (Claude's spelling) put up at a hotel in the Chaussée d'Antin. This hotel was kept by a woman, still young and good-looking, who for some years had been separated from her husband. Though she had sufficient private means, she preferred to keep the hotel, which augmented her income. But with the advent of the handsome Montgommery, she began to neglect the hotel and to look back with longing at the gay life she had once led. The Count was very *grand seigneur.* Charmed with his elegant manners, she allowed herself to be persuaded to accompany him on holiday in Italy. She was able to raise quite a sum to cover the expenses. The Count, however, insisted that, though their love should be shared, he could not take money from her and would pay his own way. A *grand seigneur* does not wish to appear a kept man. Moreover she for her part would not like her husband to think that she was a kept woman.

So off went the happy lovers on their journey to Italy. But they were never to get there. As Shakespeare says, the course of true love never did run smooth. On the way, they were staying at a hotel when, in the middle of the night, an Englishwoman presented herself at reception and demanded to see her husband who, travelling with his mistress, was to her knowledge in the hotel. The proprietor of the hotel who had taken his guests to be a married couple, ventured to announce the unexpected arrival of the Count's wife, despite the fact that the happy couple who had enjoyed a pleasant supper together were now in bed and did not wish to be disturbed. A post-chaise was waiting at the door to take the recalcitrant husband home.

Our nobleman naturally wished to avoid an embarrassing scene and a scandal, which would bring dishonour on him as well as on the lady whose husband's honour would be similarly blemished. He begged his mistress in short to make herself scarce and she, worried that the adventure might reach the ears of her husband, consented to dress quickly and disappear by a side door while the wife was waiting at the main entrance. She quickly got her things together and slipped out to find another hotel.

Having arrived at the second hotel, only then did she realise that she had left her corset behind in the first. That may not have been a major calamity, but for the fact that the same corset was literally stuffed with banknotes to the value of thirty thousand francs! But how could she go back to a scene with the Count and his wife? She had to think of the honour of her family, and of her husband. What kind of figure would she cut? So she spent a miserable night in the second hotel.

In the morning, she returned to the hastily-disturbed love-nest at the first hotel. The proprietor told her that the Englishwoman had insisted on an immediate return to England. She then asked him if he had found her corset. 'Oh, yes, Madame! The Count gave it to me when he was settling the bill.' The wretched woman was delighted. At least she was dealing with a gentleman. But, when she got back to her hotel, she found she had been doubly deceived. Her lover had played one final joke. Where she had stitched the money into the contours of her corset, it had been cut open and the banknotes were gone.

She went back to Paris a sadder and wiser woman. She took her complaint to the police and this is where Monsieur Claude comes into the story again. Having been duped himself by the English couple — for it was of course the Chief of Police of Scotland Yard *alias* the Count of Montgommery and our old friend Miss Palmer who had enacted the comedy at the hotel — he was determined to lay his hands on the pair of them.

He engaged all his aides in the search for the missing Count. It was found that his real name was Danthall; not that it mattered since he had a long list of names. Born in 1839 in Hamburg, his activities had extended over many countries on a large scale. The theft of Claude's wallet at the exhibition and the robbing of the hotel proprietress were child's play compared with the swindles he had carried out in New York, London, Spain, Monaco and Tunis, to which latter country he had fled after emptying the corset of its precious contents. It took a long time to unravel the history of the Count's misdemeanours. In Tunis he appeared to have broken with Miss Palmer. There he had gone into partnership in a bank but his partner had sought information on him in London and Paris, the police of which, now alerted, had unmasked him. Of course he was beyond their reach, and nonetheless managed to leave Tunis with part of the funds of the bank.

We next find him in Switzerland with another noble title. There he met a Frenchwoman of a certain age, as the saying goes. At her age she should have known better but she fell in love with him. Unfortunately for her, she possessed a pair of valuable diamond earrings. One day, wishing to enjoy the pleasures of nature with her new-found lover, she went with him on an expedition to Mont Blanc. She instructed the guides not to follow too closely behind and to respect their privacy. Arrived at the edge of a precipice, our noble Count removed her earrings, after which her foot happened to slip and she fell into the abyss. The guides came up and the Count reproved them for following the instructions of a silly old woman. Alone, he had been unable to save her. When Claude received the news, he guessed it was his old colleague from the exhibition and alerted the *Parquet,* but by then the noble tourist had left Switzerland.

Then we come to the final scene. A year later, who should write to Monsieur Claude but Miss Palmer, doubtlessly also sadder and wiser. In her letter she announced that, though she had been deceived by her lover, she preferred death to his abandoning her. She gave her address at a hotel near the Gare du Nord, and said that if Claude came with his agents on the morrow, she would deliver her lover to Claude even though she might have to suffer the rigours of the law with him.

As arranged, Claude went along with his bloodhounds to find a crowd at the entrance of the hotel she had indicated. One of his detectives, whom he had sent ahead, came up with the news that in the room they were to search was the dead body of a woman. She had died the previous evening. He rushed to the room and there on the floor lay the corpse of Miss Palmer. He was told that a well-dressed gentleman had been there that evening and had dinner and champagne in the room before leaving very late.

In the course of the evening, a man in a neighbouring room had heard a man's voice say, just as he was leaving. 'I hear that you have given me away, but I don't believe it. If you had, it would have been the worse for you!' Then half an hour later, a woman's voice was heard crying out, 'He's poisoned me!' Not until the morning did the man dare to knock at the door. Receiving no reply, he went to the manager who informed the police. As to the Count de Montgommery, Claude was never to have his revenge, for the Count had disappeared for good.

If we were awarding prizes in this rogues' gallery, I think the Count might be well up in the short list.

CHAPTER SIXTEEN

MURDER IN THE RUE MONSIEUR-LE-PRINCE

IN THE YEAR 1873, A CONVICT IN THE PRISON AT BREST WAS STRANGLED IN a quarrel with a fellow prisoner. His name was François Clot and at the time of his death he was serving a life sentence for murder. He might well have been guillotined since the murder was a particularly savage one which would normally call for the extreme penalty. He had a criminal record when he was apprehended and in addition the circumstances of his case provided horror, mystery and a final solution which even Dumas or Zola would have hesitated to invent.

This strange tale began in the small Normandy village of Grandchamp, where one Catherine Desmares was born in 1830. Her career from a provincial village to the splendours of a notorious courtesan's life in the Paris of the Second Empire followed a familiar pattern. It was the story of a gay life and a violent death.

She was the youngest child of a large family in reasonably comfortable circumstances. When she was fourteen her mother died. Her father took to drink and women and one may well imagine that Catherine's education, from the viewpoint of her subsequent profession, progressed rapidly as her father's mistresses succeeded one another in the house. By the time she was sixteen, she was fair game for a young Parisian spending his holidays at Grandchamp. Catherine had grown into a well-formed young woman of considerable beauty. Her full lips, her generous curves and country girl's complexion easily won the heart of Fernand Marsoulin. a young journalist and painter. They met one day in the fields, the romantic young man from the city and the awakening country girl. Nearby was a wood, which offered discreet cover for an affair of this kind, and there it all began.

Two weeks later they fled to Paris and set up house in a tiny attic in the rue Cadet. They were young, poor, in Paris and in love. They had no time to go and get married. They lived and loved. Once more we can almost hear the soft strains of *La Bohème*. A year or two later, they had abandoned the first nest in the rue Cadet and now lived in an apartment in the rue Clovis, which had been lent to them by a friend, Bernard Damès. Damès was a hanger-on in artistic circles, buying and selling paintings, lending money, collecting *objets d'art* and dabbling in all the newest enthusiasms.

It was 1848, the year of revolution. In France it was the end of the eighteen-year reign of Louis-Philippe and there was many a dry eye when he departed in some haste. The story is told that, when he and his family were about to leave the Tuileries, a man rushed forward and politely closed the carriage door for him. The King graciously thanked him and the man replied, 'I've been waiting eighteen years to do that!' In that year, not only France but the whole of Europe was in ferment, and in Paris there was fighting at the barricades. True to the romantic tradition, Fernand Marsoulin took part and got himself killed.

Catherine was left without support in the apartment in the rue Clovis. Until his death, she had been faithful to Marsoulin, but this sudden tragedy was to launch her definitely as a career woman. Damès moved in and, although she did not love him, they made a *ménage de convenance*. Meanwhile Catherine quickly widened her circle of acquaintances always with an eye on the possibility of being left alone again. This time she was determined to fall on her feet. Surely enough, Damès became involved in a swindle over some Renaissance works of art, which had very little to do with the Renaissance, and he went to prison to serve a five-year sentence. Happily the man who had been swindled was none other than the Cologne banker,

Hans Garfurth, and Catherine did fall on her feet and under the protection of Garfurth.

For seven years she was his mistress and lived in a nice house in the rue Monsieur-le-Prince. He lavished on her the usual carriages, horses, fine furniture and jewels, in fact all that Zola has depicted for us in *Nana*.

However, rich bankers who undertake to protect vigorous young girls are rarely youthful and romantic. Garfurth was getting past it, as the saying is, and his waist-line, no doubt as a result of good living with Catherine, was expanding. In 1858, he suffered an attack of apoplexy, from which he was fortunate enough to recover. His doctors issued the usual warning, so he wisely decided to abandon Catherine and his regular visits to Paris, and returned to comfortable connubial felicity in Cologne. He left Catherine the property in the rue Monsieur-le-Prince and a thousand francs a month.

Between the visits of Garfurth, Catherine had not been wasting her time and she had several friends in the background, any one of whom would have sufficed to ensure the continuation of her gay life. She even had one adventure with Napoleon III. That was of course of brief duration, as the little man was in the habit of flitting from flower to flower. Among her other clients was the Duke of Morny, the illegitimate son of Queen Hortense and hence half-brother of the Emperor. Morny, the very model of elegance in the rather flashy fashionable world of the Second Empire, was Minister of the Interior and later President of the *Corps Législatif.* He possessed an enormous fortune, obtained by anything but hard labour, which he spent on a grand scale. With such connections the village girl from Normandy had come a long way.

So, by 1863, Catherine was well advanced in her career as a

popular courtesan of the top rank, a veritable *cordon bleu* or *maillot jaune* in the world of prostitution. Her life had by no means spoiled either her looks or disposition. Her trade was to be beautiful and, above all, a woman. She never lost her head or her heart though she was certainly not cold, as her many lovers testified. She gave value for money. She was a good business-woman and for many years she made solid investments.

About that time she went on holiday to Madrid where she caught typhoid. She recovered, miraculously, despite the fact that typhoid in those days was a killer. She retained no trace of her illness and emerged as attractive as ever. In thanksgiving she rather surprisingly made a pilgrimage to Lourdes. One might have thought that the dreadful experience of her illness and the atmosphere of Lourdes might have chastened her, but it appears that she returned to Paris a nymphomaniac capable of the wildest excesses, which shocked even the bawdy society of that period. In the following year or two she plunged into a life which would have made the Emperor Nero look like an amateur.

Then she went to Italy and returned to Paris completely changed. Had she fallen in love? Had she had a child? Had she become religious, for there is none so pious as a reformed tart? Had she contracted a disease? But one had only to see her to know that she was in perfect health and as blooming as ever. She sent away her current protector, a rich Englishman, and was once again the well-balanced, sensible woman she had been before the typhoid attack.

She continued her life in the rue Monsieur-le-Prince till one day in December 1865, when the police were called to the house by her *valet de chambre,* who had gone to her room to awaken her just after dawn. On the bed lay the naked body of

Catherine Desmares. Her throat had been cut and on the rest of the body were a number of knife wounds, which could only have been inflicted by a maniac. Details of such horrors are best left in the police dossiers. In the ash tray were the remains of three small cigars. A search of the room furnished no other clues save one very strange item. Among the sumptuous lingerie which lay on the chair beside the bed, was one undergarment which, although feminine, was of inferior quality and clearly formed no part of the wardrobe of an elegant woman like Catherine Desmares. The autopsy showed that Catherine had died in perfect health. She had never borne a child and her beauty had remained unimpaired until the unknown butcher had gone to work.

The odd garment was a complete puzzle, so the police pursued their enquiries in other directions. The *femme de chambre* said that she had not shown anyone in that night and that Madame had been gay and in good spirits when she helped her to undress and left her for the night about 10.30 p.m. According to the doctors, the crime had been committed in the small hours of the morning. No one could possibly have entered the house at that time. Apart from the *femme de chambre,* the staff comprised a cook, Eva Lefranc, a woman from the same part of the country as Catherine, who had joined the household not long before, and a valet, coachman and man-of-all-work in the person of Alphonse Clergeot, who did not sleep on the premises but left at night and returned early in the morning.

The police were convinced that the crime must have been committed by a man. Clergeot, however, was able to provide a cast-iron alibi. He had played cards on the previous evening with friends and had spent the night with his mistress in the rue Vaugirard, which crosses the rue Monsieur-le-Prince.

Then suddenly the inspector in charge of the enquiry turned to Eva Lefranc, the cook, and began to undress her! The game was up. Eva admitted the crime. 'She' was a former convict on the run and the name was not Eva Lefranc but François Clot. He came from the same village as Catherine and they had grown up together. When he found her again, so many years later, he had thrown himself on her mercy. To hide him she had appointed him cook in her establishment and, in women's clothing he was secure against discovery by the police. They had apparently revived their youthful affection for one another and curiously enough, of all the lovers she had had, it was only with him that she could recapture the ecstasies she had known with Marsoulin. According to Clot she became more and more exigent.

She did not want to go on hiding him and insisted that he should resume his own identity and sex. But the ex-convict was not risking recapture. He knew he would be caught sooner or later. In the end, he lost his head and killed her in a rage. So we meet him again in the prison at Brest, where he pays the final penalty of a life for a life.

A woman might be able to understand this strange tale. No man could.

CHAPTER SEVENTEEN

VOYAGE AU PAYS
DE SIMENON

As a change from the rogues and their molls of real life, let us take a brief look at some of the villains of fiction and in particular at the work of Georges Simenon, whose enormous output never detracted from the quality of his work and whose Maigret comes to life more vividly than the real-life Monsieur Claude. Let not Simenon be dismissed, as I dismissed him many years ago when I first read him, as just another writer of whodunits. Since then, I have been among his best customers and have long lost count of the Simenons I have devoured with pleasure and profit.

Knowing French, I have been able to savour him in the original and, having lived for many years in Belgium and France, I know the background against which he writes and the kind of people he writes about. Simenon is not only a psychologist of great perception and observation but an Impressionist painter in words. In the opening pages of *L'enterrement de Monsieur Bouvet*, one is looking out of a window or the bank of the Seine early in the morning as the booksellers are just opening their displays and pinning up their prints and the first strollers are beginning their prowl for a literary bargain. The boats and barges chug along the river and one hears the sounds of Paris waking up. One suddenly realises that in a few quick strokes he has painted a picture and one has a Manet or Pissarro before one. He can conjure up a bleak landscape on a canal in Northern France as the rain streams down and Maigret waits for his man, or a backstreet in a provincial town with all its characters and gossip. And in a book such as *En Cas de Malheur*, he depicts all the frustrations of love, ambition and revenge. Above all, he can give us the authentic feel of Paris, even in translation, from the high levels of the Courts of Justice to the colour and smells of the market stalls in the rue Mouffetard.

He is obviously preoccupied with what makes people tick and he can get behind the motives not only of men but of women, something which most men find impossible. This ability of his ranges from senators to tramps and from countesses to shopgirls. In Maigret he has created a character far more real than our own cherished Sherlock Holmes. Watson is real, the average stupid man like most of us, but no one can call Holmes human. We can see Maigret off duty but what does Sherlock Holmes do when he is not being Sherlock Holmes? One can almost smell Maigret with his pipe in his stuffy office on the Quai des Orfèvres, not to mention Madame Maigret's cooking on those rare occasions when he gets home. With Maigret of course goes a fine procession of rogues and, with this in mind, I have included a short study of Simenon, which he and his wife were good enough to say they read and enjoyed immensely.

Gone are the days of the Madonna of the Sleeping Cars, when secret agents chased one another through the corridors of the Orient Express. That over-romanticised train now probably transports in one direction holiday-makers from Wigan and men from the Board of Trade carrying agreements eastwards about the rates of duty on button hooks and dolls' eyes. In the other direction it brings to us the same tired holiday-makers and gentlemen in search of British passports. Romance and mystery no longer travel on the east-west lines. They have switched to the north-south lines since Europe became Simenon country.

When the Brussels express leaves Amsterdam tonight, we know that Pietr le Letton will be on board. The Belgian police, alerted by Maigret, will observe his change of trains in Brussels and, by the time the Paris express is passing St Quentin, with whistles screaming and the rain beating on the carriage windows, there will be a dead body in one of the lavatories of the train. It will not be that of Pietr le Letton.

As you pass in the train at night through St Quentin or Charleroi or Renaix or Leuze, you see through the rain the lights of squalid houses or flats, and you know that they are packed with Simenon characters. If you could see through the steamy windows of a certain café on a street corner, you would notice a man with a cardboard suitcase, waiting for another man, a known ex-convict, to arrive from New Caledonia. Through the inner door you would see an untidy woman in a dressing gown. Simenon usually manages to get a woman in a dressing-gown in sooner or later, and the dressing-gown is always loosely tied.

It is always raining in the country of Simenon. Outside the café stands Maigret on the canal bank. It is raining so hard that it has put his pipe out. He has been there for four hours while, far away in Paris, Madame Maigret heats up the soup in vain and the famous room at the Quai des Orfèvres is simply cracking with the heat of Maigret's stove.

Meanwhile up at Brest or Le Havre or La Rochelle, a brewery is about to go bankrupt. It is a family brewery and almost every member of the family is either frustrated or mad or just waiting for the rest of the family to die. The workings of the brewery and the functions of the personnel have been given to us in that technical detail of which Simenon is a master. We could get work at the brewery on the strength of this information. We have also had the complete operation of the canal and all its locks from the source of the Marne explained to us, so that we could become lock-keepers tomorrow if we liked.

Having got thoroughly soaked, Maigret goes into the café.

'*Police Judiciaire*!' he says without taking his pipe out of his mouth. He sees in the corner a man from Delft, who has just run away with the funds of a cord and twine factory. You now know every inch of Delft and especially the Café Spruit at the corner of the Jan van Oldenbarnevelt Straat, as well as the book-keeping system of the cord and twine factory. Maigret goes to the telephone. Yes, as you rightly guessed, the head of the brewery at Brest or Le Havre or La Rochelle has been found drowned in one of his own tanks and, before you can say knife, the *Parquet* is on the job. Maigret says three words to the man with the cardboard suitcase, who is waiting for the man from New Caledonia, and nods to the *patronne,* whose dressing-gown momentarily falls open.

Maigret borrows a bicycle and follows the towpath to the railway, where the PJ have delayed the Brest, Le Havre or La Rochelle express. Maigret sleeps in his soaking clothes. On arrival at Brest, Le Havre or La Rochelle, he puts up at the *Cheval Blanc.* He sends the boots out to buy a shirt and collar and washes his hands and face, Maigret never takes a bath. Having dried his clothes, he goes into the rain again, for it is always raining in Brest or Le Havre or La Rochelle.

He is shown into the family home of the brewers. Here follows a complete inventory of the heavy mahogany furniture. The brewer's family appear to resent Maigret. He says '*Police Judiciaire*!' and they recoil. He telephones the *Parquet* and asks them to send on the finger-prints of Pietr le Letton. He also asks for the family history of the man with the cardboard suitcase, who is waiting for the man from New Caledonia in the café in St Quentin or Charleroi.

At this moment a fishing boat arrives from Iceland. On it is the brewer's long-dead brother, who is not really dead at all, though he will be when Pietr le Letton gets his hands on him. But we anticipate. In the meantime, in a coal-miner's cottage in Liège, a young man with a red nose, who wants to marry the coal-miner's daughter, who has been doing a spell in a night-club in Marseilles, is hiding in a bedroom. He has a cold, because it is raining in Liège and he has had to walk all the way from the station in patent-leather shoes. He has murdered a man on the Basle express, thus maintaining the north-south line tradition. He, too, had a cardboard suitcase, packed with money he has stolen from the man on the Basle express. About this time, the police in New Caledonia have received a cable from the Quai des Orfèvres. They do nothing, as the local chief of police is in a café with the *patronne,* who is a half-caste in a dressing-gown, which keeps falling open because she will not tie it up properly.

While all this has been going on, Maigret has smoked and refilled his pipe forty-three times. Madame Maigret has been packing so that she and Maigret can take a holiday with her sister in Alsace or Lorraine or Seine Inférieure or wherever she is. But they will never have that holiday, for Maigret has left Brest or Le Havre or La Rochelle for Delft. Madame Maigret doesn't mind. She is used to this, and it is raining anyway.

Maigret has now got his men posted in the rain at St Quentin, Charleroi, Liège, Brest, Le Havre and La Rochelle, and in each town the *Parquet* has been alerted. The miner's wife in Liège is getting worried about her lodger with the red nose, and she very rightly wonders where her daughter earns such a princely salary. Certainly not as a sales girl in the *Galeries du Boulevard Anspach,* where she says she works. She surprises the young man who is literally covered with blood-stained bank-notes upstairs in bed. His cold is getting worse.

Now, where is Maigret? He is just coming out of the station in Delft. At the café opposite, the cashier of the cord and twine factory used to play billiards with the Mayor, the local magistrate or a man closely resembling Pietr le Letton every Wednesday at nine o'clock. It is now Thursday and half-past five, and raining into the bargain. Maigret sends the waiter out to buy a new shirt and collar, and washes his face, presumably with the pipe in his mouth.

A billiards game is in progress. A mysterious Englishman in tweeds and a deerstalker, called Sir Charles Dickens, is playing the local brewer. For the rest of the story he will be known as Sir Dickens. Sir Dickens is drunk, but is playing a good game. Maigret goes to the telephone and rings the Quai des Orfèvres and Interpol. He learns that Lepine the Leopard is on the Hamburg-Cologne express. He has the train halted at Bad Faulstein. No trace of Pietr le Letton on board, but a body falls out of one of the lavatories. His pockets are stuffed with brewery shares from the brewery at Brest, Le Havre or La Rochelle. In his hand is a ticket from Delft to New Caledonia.

Next morning Maigret is at the Quai des Orfèvres, looking out at the train, stoking the fire in the filthy stove in the centre of the room, filling his pipe and sending out for clean shirts, glasses of beer and ham sandwiches. Lepine the Leopard is now in Paris. He has arrived by way of Cologne and Brussels. He is in a café in the rue des Brocanteurs, talking to a woman in a dressing-gown in a back room. Yes, the dressing-gown keeps falling open. Her brother is not in New Caledonia after all. He proves to be none other than the hatmaker of Vitry-le-François.

While we are talking, one of Maigret's men, still standing in the rain by the Iceland fishing-boat at Brest, Le Havre or La Rochelle, has recognised the stranger from Reykjavik. He is not

171

the brother of the brewer, but the long-lost husband of the Seven Mad Women of Argenteuil, as you will probably have guessed by now. Twenty four hours later, the body of the woman in the café in the rue des Brocanteurs is found in the Seine by a bargee at Charenton. Upstream, you notice. Who is she? Sir Dicken's wife? Let us ask Maigret, who has scarcely opened his mouth except to take out his pipe and say '*Police Judiciaire!*' in the last two hundred pages. Where is he? The room at the Quai des Orfèvres, where the fug is so thick you can cut it with a knife, is empty. At this moment Maigret is standing in the rain outside the miner's cottage in Liège.

From a window farther up the street a frustrated spinster is watching him through the curtains. In the wardrobe behind her is, who knows? Pietr le Letton? Maigret's pipe has gone out. The miner's wife opens the door. '*Police Judiciaire!*' says Maigret and walks in past her. As he expected, there in the corner sits, but of course, you will have guessed.

At this stage I had better assure you that in another fifty pages or so Simenon will have tied all this up and you can relax.

CHAPTER EIGHTEEN

PATOURON AND THE FARMER'S WIFE

TOWARDS THE END OF 1873, THE SEINE WAS IN FLOOD AND LARGE AREAS OF Paris were inundated. Monsieur Claude's police force was transformed overnight into a river police. They patrolled the streets of Paris, now like Venetian canals, in boats by day and night, rescuing families suddenly trapped in the upper floors of their houses. It even looked as if the bridges would be flooded. In fact the high water mark can still be seen on some of the Seine bridges. Debris floated all over the vast sheet of water which the centre of Paris had become, and the flood washed out many a dark secret.

One man was by his name and nature in his true element and that was Claude's inspector Requin, the Shark, whom we have already met, with his flair for corpses in the affair of the female Cyclops. He worked round the clock, not only rescuing the living but fishing out the dead, the accidentally drowned and the murdered. One day the body of a coachman in the Canal Saint-Martin; on another he pulled a woman's body out of the water near the Quai Jemappes. They were both obviously the victims of crimes. Though eventually identified, their killers were never found.

Requin had a more spectacular catch near the Quai d'Orsay. Assisted by Bagasse and La Fouine, two other star bloodhounds of Claude's, he landed the body of a man of about fifty. The man was gagged, his legs were bent double and firmly strapped together and his hands were tied behind his back. There was no doubt at all about foul play here. It could not have been a pretty sight as the body had been in the water for several weeks and it was only the flood water which had washed it out to such a public place as the Quai d'Orsay. A photograph of the body, just as it was found, was posted up but no one was able to identify the man or give any clue to the mystery. The case

174

would have reposed in the closed files of the police, had it not been for another crime discovered later.

On the edge of a wood in one of the districts to the west of Paris, near the Breil farm at a place called the *Carrefour du poirier de Judas,* the Judas-tree Crossroads, people from the local village found a man lying dead. The body was lying face downwards, but two large gaping wounds could be seen near the right temple. He was lying in a pool of blood. The face was so disfigured as to be unrecognisable. All that could be said was that he had been dead for several hours. News of the discovery quickly reached the Breil farm and the farmer's wife hastened to the spot. She looked at the body. 'Idiots!' said she, 'can't you see it's my husband? He must have killed himself by accident. He was too fond of going off hunting!' No tears, no distress. Such an outburst did not make a very good impression on those standing around. It had been known for some time that the farmer's wife disliked him and preferred the company and attentions of one of the farm workers named Patouron, a character of doubtful antecedents. The farmer on the other hand was a kind and honourable fellow, whose misfortune it was to be married to such a trollop. From the very beginning, when this Patouron had been engaged, a *ménage à trois* had been formed and had continued for four years, though the good-natured farmer of course had no idea that Patouron was his wife's lover. The wife had always insisted on how indispensible Patouron was in the work of the farm and the farmer had come to believe her. She, being much younger than her husband, was so sure of herself and carried on the affair so openly that everyone knew what was going on except the trusting husband.

Thus, when the farmer's brother came to spend a few days at the farm, it was not long before he saw how his brother was being fooled. He took his sister-in-law to task. He told her quite firmly, 'If you do not break off the liaison with this farm worker, I shall inform my brother for the honour of our family. Now I'm going, because I do not want to be a witness to this scandal any longer; but if, at Gentilly, I do not receive a letter from you announcing the departure of your lover, I intend to write to my brother and tell him everything I have seen and heard here. You had better see to it. You have been warned!' And off he went to Gentilly where he lived. He was a very different type from his brother. While the farmer was trusting and kind, the brother was a man of action who stood for no nonsense.

The wife of course was furious and rushed off to tell her lover of the threat to their dalliance. He realised that something had to be done — and quickly at that — if the love affair was to go on. 'I know your brother-in-law,' he said, 'and he'll do what he says. We are never going to be parted so we've got to deal with him before we get rid of your husband. Let's get over to Gentilly quick!' They found a plausible pretext to go off together. The brother-in-law had hardly got back to his home before the wife and the lover arrived.

Patouron told him that, if he did not keep his mouth shut, it would cost him his life. The brother-in-law was naturally outraged and threatened to denounce them at once to his brother so that he could get rid of them both. That was enough for the gentle lovers. They both attacked at once. Patouron stabbed him and the wife, who had thoughtfully brought a rope with her, helped to gag and tie him up. Patouron then finished him off by stabbing him again and again.

As the victim lived alone and the place where he lived was remote, they had no difficulty in getting rid of the body, which they threw into the Bièvre, a tributary of the Seine. They little thought that the coming flood would deliver it as far as the Quai d'Orsay into the hands of our old friend Requin, who, when he discovered it had no idea who had committed the murder.

So the *ménage à trois* was resumed at the Breil farm and life went on as before. The next step was of course to get rid of the farmer. Patouron decided to poison him. One very warm day, he offered his master a glass of lemonade. Mixed in it was a quantity of phosphorus obtained from matches and two poisonous insects of unknown species! Compared with the efficiency he had shown in the murder and disposal of the brother-in-law, this seemed rather an amateurish effort, and so it proved. The farmer drank up and suffered not the least inconvenience The wife and Patouron were stupified. They would have to begin all over again.

As the farmer was getting worried at having no news from his brother at Gentilly, and as he would most certainly be able to throw some light on his fate when the disappearance became known, our two lovers had to act quickly. Together they proposed a little shooting excursion to the farmer. What about a trip to the Judas-tree Crossroads for some game? So Patouron and the farmer set off.

Patouron, helpful and attentive as ever, offered to load the farmer's gun for him and rammed the charge so that the gun would explode. The farmer would then conveniently kill himself. Guided to the spot by Patouron, the farmer took a shot, and nothing happened. Patouron was in a rage. First the lemonade and now this! He raised his own gun and, instead of aiming at any passing game, he got his master in the sights. He shot him in the ear but even this did not kill him. Murder can be a frustrating business at times. Later, at the trial, he was to say, 'Ah he appeared to be in pain and suffering terribly, I thought I'd be doing him a good turn by giving him another shot at close range!' So he had given him another in the face which rendered him unrecognisable.

There he lay, till a few hours later, the wife arrived on the arm of Patouron with her cry of 'You idiots! it's my husband!'

From that point it was not difficult to get to the bottom of the affair. The farmer's gun had been charged with paper torn from a school book *Le Petit Jean,* which was found locked in a box belonging to Patouron. At the Assizes he ran true to form. He told the judges, 'I have no regret for what I have done. If he were still alive, I'd kill him again.'

Patouron was clearly a bad lot. He had been in trouble before and had served a prison sentence. As to the wife, charged with him, she claimed at the trial that she was innocent and had nothing to do with the murder of her husband or that of her brother-in-law. She defied the court to prove that she had made the journey to Gentilly and had helped to throw the body into the Bièvre. As far as the death of the husband was concerned, she said that Patouron had threatened to kill her if she informed on him.

The President of the court was not impressed. He summed the whole affair up, addressing himself to the wife, from the time she became Patouron's mistress through the four-year liaison which was then getting precarious, to the intervention of the brother-in-law and the second murder arising inevitably from the first. 'You were united,' he said, 'as much by murder as by adultery! Don't deny it, *femme Breil,* you were Patouron's mistress!' There was no nonsense about the President's determination to pin them both down and he pulled out all the

stops. 'I do not deny it!' said the *femme Breil,* heroic in her love
for a moment. 'And did you say,' pursued the President, 'that
if Breil died, you would marry him?' 'No, it's not true!' she
cried, trying to draw back. 'Good! the case is clear.' said the
President, turning to Patouron. 'Your mistress put you up to
the crimes and you carried them out.'

There was no doubt about the verdict. Patouron was sentenced to death and the farmer's wife to penal servitude for life.
When one considers what prison life was like a hundred years
ago, Patouron probably got off best. At the time of the sentences, the wife was twenty two and Patouron barely twenty
three.

CHAPTER NINETEEN

BECKER
THE FORGER

THIS IS AN ENTIRELY DIFFERENT KIND OF ROGUE, A GIFTED AND likeable character, who devoted his life to counterfeiting yet never saw the inside of a prison and was never bothered by the police. Before examining the life of Carl Wilhelm Becker and his work, let us look at a subject which interests us all, money.

Money as we know it was invented as recently as the seventh century BC. The first coins were said to have been made by the Lydians. In any case it is generally agreed that money originated in Asia Minor about that time. Such is the wickedness of mankind, forgery was invented shortly afterwards. As soon as anything acquires a value there will always be someone to imitate it. During the first years of the occupation of Germany after the Second World War, it was said that, on the day of issue of a temporary form of currency for the use of the occupation forces, large quantities of the forged variety were similarly ready for circulation in Hamburg. However, there is no doubt that the wonderful new purchasing power of the first coins of gold, silver and electrum inspired the earliest forgers to make their own. Do-it-yourself moneymaking is as old as that.

From early Greek and Roman times forgers have been at work and fairly frequently moulds for the production of false coins have been discovered in archaeological excavations. There are two kinds of forgery. One which counterfeits coins in current use and the other which imitates valuable ancient coins in order to deceive collectors and souvenir-hunters.

Forgery has always been a heavily punished crime. Even today, when our money is hardly worth counterfeiting, the amateur maker of notes and coin is sure of a stiff sentence. To give one example, forgery in the fifteenth century was considered a usurpation of royal prerogative, quite apart from the

182

matter of upsetting the national economy. In the town of Tours in France in 1486, a jeweller and a priest were charged with forging coins. The priest could not be dealt with by the secular court and he was handed over to the ecclesiastical authority, but the jeweller was condemned to be boiled alive and then hung in a public place. A great pot was set up in the market place so that all could enjoy the spectacle. The unfortunate jeweller was trussed up and thrown into the boiling water. Twice he came to the surface only to be thrust under again by the executioner. A third time he came up with his arms free. He screamed for mercy as the executioner tried to beat him down again. Then the crowd turned against the executioner and, after a frightful struggle, the wretched forger was rescued from the pot, still alive, and carried to a church where he claimed sanctuary. Later, in the seventeenth century, forgers were simply hanged.

Forgery can be truly an art, requiring taste, skill and technical knowledge. In the late Renaissance in Italy, bronze medals were made in imitation of Ancient Roman *sestertii*. The *sestertius* was a bronze coin about the size of an old penny but a little thicker. Many of them are very handsome pieces with fine portraits of the emperors and their families. The Italian imitations by such well-known artists as Cavino and Bassiano are called Paduans and are easy to detect. They nevertheless have quite a value of their own as works of art of the period.

Of a much more dangerous type were the forgeries of Carl Wilhelm Becker. He was born in Speyer in Germany in 1772, the son of a vineyard and wine business proprietor who was a town councillor and local pillar of society. In his youth he had no wish to go into his father's trade and expressed an ambition to become a sculptor. Papa Becker did not like this idea at all and sent him off to study the wine trade at Bordeaux.

Nevertheless he is said to have started drawing ancient coins and cutting dies even then, but the wine trade seems to have held him since in 1795, when at the age of twenty-three, he was in that business in Frankfurt. In that year he married. The wine trade palled for him and he changed to drapery. That too failed and we find him in 1803 in Speyer, Mannheim and finally Munich where he managed to get a job at the Royal Mint. There he learned the art of engraving steel dies and his life's work really began.

Now in the seventeenth and eighteenth centuries the possession and maintenance of a private *cabinet de médailles* was considered to be one of the attributes of a gentleman. Such a pastime well fitted a man of breeding and scholarship. To build up a collection of Greek and Roman coins called for a classical education, taste and, of course, wealth. As many of those who made the grand tour brought back pictures and other antiquities from all over Europe to found some of the great collections of today, so others gathered fine specimens of the coins of Ancient Rome and Greece for their cabinets. The connoisseurs of those days were a far cry from some of the so-called numismatists of today who, with their Victorian bun pennies have little knowledge of history and collect on rarity value alone or else buy precious coins purely as an investment. It is ironical that, as our own currency declines in value, the moneys of the Ancient World increase in value at a steadier rate than do industrial shares.

Greek and Roman coins are often objects of great beauty such as the silver decadrachms of Syracuse, minor masterpieces of the classical period of Greek art, or the superb portraits in miniature of the emperors on Roman gold, silver and bronze coins of the first two centuries of the Christian era. They were prized by the artist for their aesthetic value and by the scholar and historian as important historical sources. Indeed it has been said that a large part of our knowledge of the ancients comes to us through coinage, on which were inscribed lasting records of great men and events, religious and sporting festivities, remissions of taxes, harvests and other matters to do with the economy as well as military campaigns and conquests.

Thus there was a great demand for fine pieces which commanded considerable prices. It was this market which Becker, from his studies at the Munich mint and experiments at home together with his knowledge of the ancient coinages, worked and studied to supply. In following Becker's career, it is clear that he was not only activated by the need to make a living; he was also able to indulge these loves of his life, the appreciation of the masterpieces of the ancient coin makers and his skill in engraving dies.

Before 1810, he was already making imitations of Greek silver coins. In that year he undertook a trip to Switzerland and Italy and in Milan he sold some coins to a famous collection, whose director recommended him to other collectors. The director in Milan later complained that Becker had deceived him but, since no action was taken, it is conceivable that Becker started off with genuine coins for sale. There is nothing like a little ground bait.

Though it was generally known, as the years went by, that Becker was making excellent imitations of Greek, Roman and other coins in silver and gold, he appears to have avoided prosecution. No collector or museum director likes to announce in public that he has been deceived and that his judgment is at fault. It is remarkable that, during this period, when Becker lived in Mannheim, he was doing business with the

Rothschilds. They were not only bankers but dealers in coins. In fact today a well-known bank in Zurich has regular sales of coins. One cannot think that the Rothschilds were easy to fool. In 1812, Becker was back in the wine business in Frankfurt, possibly to tide him over a difficult period, but this did not last long and soon he was to devote the rest of his life to producing a series of imitations of Greek, Roman, Visigothic, French, German and other coins as well as commemorative medals of historical importance.

He must have been an engaging personality. He became friendly with Prince Carl von Isenburg, who gave him the title of *Hofrat* (Court Councillor). Even Goethe sought him out, having heard of him as a gentleman collector willing to dispose of fine pieces and other antiques. That Goethe gave him a copy, dedicated in his own hand, of his translation of *The Life of Benvenuto Cellini,* is an indication of his esteem for him as an amateur of art.

People continued to talk of Becker's imitations. One famous collector, on whom Becker attempted to pass off three allegedly ancient coins, had a most diplomatic correspondence with him in which he gently pointed out that it was regrettable that such a connoisseur as Becker could have been deceived. Becker was only too willing to offer to take them back and substitute coins which were genuine beyond doubt. It looks as if Becker used to get away with it if he could with his beautiful imitations, but he always left a loop-hole through which he could emerge with dignity and an alternative offer, probably of genuine pieces.

He seems to have had a life of ups and downs, no less in his business than in his home life. He was divorced in 1822, married again and then the second marriage broke down. In Vienna he married for a third time. In 1824, he had accumulated a magnificent collection of dies of his own making, dating from Greek and Roman times to the seventeenth century. He then had the temerity to offer them to the Imperial Coin Cabinet in Vienna. One cannot help sensing a suspicion of blackmail in this. Any honest collector, from the keepers of the Imperial collections downwards, would have been happy to see such dangerous dies in safekeeping. While there were people like Becker about, every new acquisition had to be doubly scrutinised. Metternich himself gave instructions that the offer should be considered. This led to a lot of undignified haggling and in the end the offer at Becker's price was refused.

In Vienna, Becker was in touch, and often on terms of friendship, with many famous collectors and experts. He still made dies and dealt in all manner of antiques. But he left Vienna rather suddenly and returned to Germany, possibly as the place was getting too hot for him. The offer to sell his dies and the continued circulation of false pieces, however good their workmanship, might have led to closer enquiries and prosecution.

Then in 1825, appeared a pamphlet by an Italian numismatist called Sestini, warning collectors of Becker's forgeries. Becker, he admitted, said that he only made his copies of rare coins to fill gaps in collections when genuine pieces could not be obtained, but he also accused Becker of trying to sell his dies when he saw that the game was up. On Becker's side and to his advantage was the unwillingness of experts to admit their mistakes. There were also probably some dealers who, knowing they were handling first-class imitations, passed them on to others, dealers and collectors, as genuine. It was worth it. A set of Becker's coins, if sold as genuine, could make an enormous profit.

Becker continued his frantic buying and selling of pictures and antiques but he seems to have been in financial difficulties. He was a great artist but a bad business-man, I suspect. When he died in 1830, he left his family largely unprovided for. While the dies were at large, so to speak, there was danger for the collector, and eventually the famous — or should we say notorious — dies ended up in the Saalburg Museum. In 1911, they were acquired for the Kaiser Friedrich Museum in Berlin.

However much we praise Becker's knowledge and skill, there is no doubt that his activities occasioned wholesale mischief in the world of numismatics. People began to look at their collections more closely. Experts in those days did not have the knowledge which we have and many of his creations which today would be suspect must have been considered genuine. Even how, some might get by, having acquired the patina of a century and a half.

Nevertheless they are a magnificent achievement. Sir George Hill, who published his *Becker the Counterfeiter* in 1924, established a reliable guide book to Becker's forgeries with a set of plates which are both a tribute to Becker's skill and a warning to collectors at the same time.

That Becker was a rogue, however dedicated he may have been to his art and the study of the ancient coinages, is practically certain. One point more than any other which tells against him is the story that he was in the habit of taking the newness off his finished coins — since very few ancient coins are found in completely mint condition — by putting them in a box fixed to the axle of his carriage and going for a drive. Thus they were shaken up thoroughly on the roads of that time and given the appearance of having been slightly used. There are entries in his diary to the effect that he had 'taken his coins for a ride!'

Becker compares well with some of our other rogues. After all, he did go to a lot of trouble and exercised all his skill and knowledge, which were considerable, to deceive us.

CHAPTER TWENTY

THE MURDERER
FROM METZ

ON 2ND DECEMBER 1873, THE POLICE OF MONTMARTRE WERE CALLED TO AN apartment on the fourth floor of a house in the rue Audran, the home of a secondhand dealer. He had been murdered in a particularly brutal manner. A mattress and an eiderdown had been thrown over the body which was horribly mutilated. There were about fifty wounds inflicted with a knife of some kind. The skull had been smashed with a blunt instrument and the head was almost severed from the body. A hammer and a razor lay beside the corpse. Various drawers in the room had been forced, and the dead man's son, who had called the police to break open the door, said that eight thousand francs in gold and banknotes as well as twelve negotiable bonds of the City of Paris were missing.

At this point Monsieur Claude and his faithful inspector Lynx-Eye arrived. The latter at once lived up to his reputation. He managed to find a piece of newspaper and a fragment of an envelope stained with blood on the floor. The newspaper bore the name of a printer in Metz and the envelope was postmarked from that city.

The secondhand dealer came from Metz and had the unusual name of Faath. Like many other inhabitants of Alsace and Lorraine, after those two provinces had passed into German hands he came to Paris to live near his son, a young architect. A widower, he lived on his own, though the son came every evening except Sunday to dine with him.

The doctor said that the crime had probably been committed a day or two earlier, on the Sunday, the day when the son did not visit his father. This suggested that the murderer knew the victim's habits. It was likely that he too came from Metz since the fragment of paper might have fallen or been torn from the murderer's pocket in a struggle.

The police had little information to work on. Faath had only recently arrived from Metz. He lived a quiet well-ordered life and did not mix. He went out only to the stock exchange occasionally or to buy furniture for his stock at the public auctions. The son too led a life as regular and uneventful as his father. For some days the police made no progress at all. There were no known criminals from Metz who might have been in touch with Faath. At the autopsy it was thought that, from the extreme violence with which the murder was carried out, it could only have been committed by someone accustomed to handling heavy tools such as a blacksmith or woodcutter. Beyond that the crime presented a complete mystery.

Then, a few days later, the police arrested in the street a woman who had been acting very strangely and who at first was thought to be mad. Taken to the police station she put on an act which sounded like a variation of the part of Lady Macbeth in its preoccupation with bloodstains. All she could say was: 'Gold, gold to wash the blood from your clothes! No! No! Boudas' wife will never wash the clothes of an assassin at that price! Go away, Boudas, go away!' She was taken over by Monsieur Claude and he judged that, from her accent, she was from Lorraine. His intuition, which incidentally was rarely wrong, told him that he might have got hold of the wife of Faath's murderer.

Realising that she was, at least temporarily, out of her mind as the result of some appalling shock, he decided to get at the truth by frightening her rather than trying to reason with her. Putting on a Metz accent, he pretended to be the husband coming to her with his hands full of money and his clothes all bloodstained, asking her to wash off the evidence of his crime. She reacted as he expected, crying out again to Boudas to go back to Metz, that she was his wife but would never be his accomplice in washing his clothes. Claude was convinced that he had there the wife of the murderer from Metz. As indeed he had.

The probability that the murderer came from that part of the country was confirmed to some extent by the concierge of the house in the rue Audran. He told Claude that an unknown man had been there on the Sunday and had enquired where Faath lived. He said that the man spoke with an Alsatian accent. That was near enough though Metz happens to be in Lorraine. The concierge was not able to see the man's features and, when he left about an hour later, he again could not see what he looked like. On the assumption that the murderer had gone back to Metz, Claude despatched his own secretary at once to make enquiries there, and sent Lynx-Eye round to Boudas' home. True to his nickname again, Lynx-Eye missed nothing. He gave the Boudas residence a good going-over and returned in triumph with further fragments of the envelope, part of which he had found at the rue Audran. He had found them in the pocket of a jacket which appeared to have been cleaned recently. This was a definite link. He also learned that Boudas had not been back since the night of the crime.

Claude's secretary was not so lucky in Metz. All he could discover was that Boudas had been there at the banking house of Mayer on 1st December to cash the stolen bonds. Boudas had apparently left Paris late on the Sunday night. On the Monday Mayer had paid him one thousand five hundred francs on account against the bonds pending their negotiation on the Paris Stock Exchange. There was no other trace of Boudas.

Faath's son in the meantime had tried to put a stop on the payment of the bonds, of which he happened to have the numbers, but Boudas had been too quick for him. Bearer bonds can be negotiated by anyone. It later transpired that Boudas, having got his advance from Mayer, left for Brussels. The secretary in Metz, and Lynx-Eye in Paris, got no further in their enquiries and several months went by without trace of the murderer anywhere.

Then, by a lucky chance, Lynx-Eye's colleague, Requin the Shark happened on a trail which finally led to the arrest of Boudas. It was through a woman. If I were asked what advice I would give to successful thieves and murderers to enable them to avoid the arm of the law, I would recommend them not to spend their ill-gotten gains on women. I have studied many causes of crime over many years and again and again the final arrest has been due to a woman. Sometimes the criminal overspends his newly-acquired wealth and the sudden appearance of his moll, decked out in jewellery and new clothes, draws undue attention to him. When jealousy comes into it, his arrest is even more certain. He buys his wife or mistress a mink coat or some articles of jewellery, which rouse the jealousy of another woman, whose lover or husband has not been so successful or generous; or, worse still, he has two molls and buys for one more than he buys for the other. This leads to talk and this is the kind of talk the police love to hear. Boudas was no exception to the rule and it duly led him to the six o'clock walk.

To get back to Requin, we are in the early months of 1874, when the Shark happened to arrest a whore, who had been fighting with one of her colleagues in a cheap dance hall. The woman, whose name was Bonhaert, came from Brussels. It appeared that the fight took place because the other woman refused to have anything to do with Bonhaert. She had accused her of associating only with criminals and of having more money than she could have earned in the honest pursuit of her profession.

By chance more than anything else, Claude decided to interrogate the woman Bonhaert and here again his instinct was right. She told him that the cause of the fight arose from her acquaintance with an odd character from Metz, who had come to Paris and taken her out of the bordello where she worked, to accompany him on his travels. He was an ugly brute, she said, but he had his pockets filled with gold. He had spent one night with her and had paid the madame of the house to allow the woman to leave with him.

He first took her to Lille but he could not stay long in any place. No sooner were they in Lille, than he took her off to Metz. And, as soon as they got to Metz, they were on their way to Brussels. All the time he drank like a fish and behaved in a most peculiar way. After two months of this wandering, she had had enough. He paid her off and she left him to return to her old haunts in Paris, where she did not get a very warm welcome from her colleagues, who were possibly jealous.

Bonhaert was able to give Claude a good description of Boudas. This was at last something to work on and finally, in the criminal archives of the Metz region, he came upon a photograph of Boudas and his record. He was an ex-convict who had been sentenced in 1854 for the theft of cheques from a business firm near Metz. He had also worked as a woodcutter and sawyer, which is what the police had guessed at the time of the murder. Now Claude believed that criminals always return to the scene of their original crime and once again he sent his secretary to Metz in the belief that Boudas would eventually turn up there. In fact Boudas had in due course returned from Brussels to Metz. Claude also sent inspectors to all the places to which Boudas had dragged the woman Bonhaert. Anyway, after a most complicated manhunt, Boudas was arrested in May 1874, nearly six months after the crime in the rue Audran.

He proved to be as ugly and repulsive a brute as his photograph and the description given by the woman indicated. Claude says he was such a monster that he inspired pity rather than terror. It is a curious feature of this case that Boudas seems to have been overcome by remorse after the murder of Faath and to have been fleeing from the horror of his crime as he moved restlessly from place to place. He had gone home that evening and his wife had been horrified at his appearance, covered with blood and with his pockets full of gold. When she refused to clean him up, he beat her till she washed his clothes. But the events of that night caused her to lose her reason. He left Paris at a late hour and on the Monday morning was at Metz waiting for the bank to open.

It was Faath's misfortune to have got to know Boudas. They were in Metz together at the time of the siege of that fortress in the war of 1870 and since then Boudas had not lost track of Faath. He had kept in touch with him in Paris as a fellow exile from the homeland and it was on the pretext of a mutually profitable business deal that he had gained admittance to Faath's apartment that night. But after the crime he found himself unable to stay in one place and he could not live alone. Before taking up with the woman Bonhaert, he had had another woman trailing round with him.

Once in the hands of the police, he never ceased to proclaim his innocence and nothing would shake him. There was no witness to the crime; the concierge at the rue Audran could not identify him; only his wife could be called against him and she was now mad and unfit to give evidence. When he was shown the weapons, the razor and the hammer, he said they were just secondhand stuff from Faath's stock and nothing to do with him. In fact the defence even called a cutler to prove that the razor was an antique. But the envelope fragments at both his home and at the rue Audran, together with the cashed bonds, told against him.

Asked how he had acquired the bonds, he said he had found them. 'Exactly,' said the President of the court, 'you "found" them just as you "found" the cheques in 1854 when you were sent to prison then!' No reply from Boudas. 'Well, supposing you did find those bonds at Metz, how do you explain your strange behaviour with these women whom you terrified?' Boudas found a reply which seemed to embarrass the judge. 'When you're out with the girls, Monsieur le Président, you're not on your best behaviour, as you yourself know!' However, he still continued to protest that he was innocent in the prison of La Roquette after he had been sentenced to death.

Claude visited him in the condemned cell, always hoping for a confession. 'It's my ugly mug which has done for me!' he repeatedly told Claude. 'I may be a thief but I'm not a murderer!' Claude said that he had the face of a wild beast, a man of the woods where he had plied his trade as a woodcutter. He had a full beard, bristling in all directions, and a brutish receding forehead. A real wolf, according to Claude.

The execution of Boudas was a sensational event. He was guillotined together with an entirely different kind of rogue, Moreau the pharmacist and poisoner, whose story we relate before we meet the two of them in the last scene in front of the prison of La Roquette.

CHAPTER TWENTY-ONE

MOREAU, PHARMACIST AND POISONER

IT IS A STRANGE FACT THAT QUITE A NUMBER OF CRIMINALS HAVE BEGUN their careers in a seminary. The first one which springs to mind is Fouché, possibly the greatest of them all. Then there was Talleyrand, an able man of many parts but well qualified for any rogues' gallery. Another, of a different stamp, was Frederick Rolfe, self-styled Baron Corvo, of Hadrian the Seventh fame. The specimen we are about to examine is one more example, Pierre-Désiré Moreau. He was born at Châteaudun, the son of a peasant who was unable to give him any education. At the time of his crimes he was proprietor of what we would call a herbalist's shop at Saint-Denis near Paris. He had come a long way by the time he was thirty-two years old.

He had been a bright little boy, so bright that a priest had taken an interest in him and decided to educate him. He did this with such success and the pupil showed such promise that he sent him to a seminary. Little did the good priest know that he had set him on a career which was to end on the guillotine in the Place de la Roquette. At the seminary the young Moreau astonished his teachers by his intelligence, but neither the cloister nor the presbytery were for him. Before long he had thrown overboard any aspiration to the priesthood and was on his way. He had other ideas of making a fortune.

He started badly by deciding to marry a woman of no means. However her parents showed no enthusiasm for Moreau as a son-in-law and for the time being the marriage was off, so he enlisted in the army and served six years. Meanwhile Mademoiselle Aubry, his *fiancée*, waited like Penelope for his return. They were married for three-and-a-half years when she died. That was in 1873 and she was thirty-three years old. Moreau had been studying, after his return from military service, to be a pharmacist and was about to pass his finals, having made a special study of poisons. As it later appeared, he had applied this special study to the murder of his wife.

The report placed before the tribunal, when he was finally brought to book, sums up the whole affair and needs no further comment:

> On 18th August 1873, Madame Moreau died at Saint-Denis, aged thirty-three, following a brief illness. She had been married for three-and-a-half years to the accused, a herbalist by profession. It was he who, in his capacity as a student of pharmacy, took upon himself the preparation of the medicines and the small amount of food she was able to take. From the beginning to the end of her illness she was vomiting incessantly and in great pain. Despite the doctor's recommendation, Moreau took care to see that no vomited matter should be preserved. Finally, on her death, Moreau announced that she had died from a malady of the stomach. On 16th August, two days before her death, the pharmacist had taken his wife to a lawyer in Saint-Denis and she had made a will in her husband's favour leaving him all she possessed.

As his wife died, Moreau threw himself into a chair, crying out to Madame Aubry, his mother-in-law, 'If only you knew how we loved one another! What is to become of me?'

He was not worried for long. Soon after, he was having an affair with a married woman, but this had to be broken off in view of his plans to marry again. This time it was a certain Mademoiselle Lagneau. As her name unhappily implied, here was a second lamb for the slaughter.

Mademoiselle Lagneau, who was thirty-one, had been living in sin for twelve years with a Paris business-man. However, with a chance of being made an honest woman by Moreau, she

201

offered a dowry of twenty-five thousand francs, a small house and the furniture of her former lover who appeared to be quite happy to pay this price for getting rid of her. Moreau had no scruples in thus taking over the wages of sin. This second wife was not a delicate little flower like the first one. Nevertheless, despite her normally robust health, she fell ill only just over eight months after the demise of the other. Moreau was not one to let the grass grow under his feet. She had the same symptoms as her predecessor and, after thirteen days of vomiting, she died a similar death. In this case too all medicines and all food and drink had been prepared by the devoted husband. Moreau took the precaution of having a different doctor this time. One does not want too many coincidences in the family. This doctor, who seems to have been no more observant than the first, diagnosed what he called diphtheric angina, though he admitted that he could not account for the persistent vomiting.

Some days before her death, the second Madame Moreau had expressed a wish for a steak, which Moreau duly bought and cut in two. He cooked one half and served it to his wife. She ate a mouthful and gave the rest to the servant. The servant, remembering that Moreau had said his wife was getting worse, brought the steak to him. He took it and was careful to get rid of it at once in the refuse. Though he knew his wife was dying, he did not inform her family till she was beyond help. When her mother and sister arrived, she was on the point of death. A few days earlier, she was beginning to suspect that she was being poisoned and said so to a visiting cousin. When told of this, Moreau said she must be wandering in her mind. She repeated her fears to the servant and, finally, an hour before she died, when her cousin and her cousin's husband came to see her, she said, 'Moreau has poisoned me!'

Moreau shed no tears but his wife's last words had done for him. It remained to be proved how the deaths of the two wives had come about. Both bodies were exhumed and it was seen at autopsy that the first wife had had no stomach trouble and that the second had not died from diphtheric angina, so we have two doctors with red faces. Traces of copper were found in both bodies and it was clear that an emetic of some kind had been used to poison them.

Moreau had been studying poisons for some time. Among the material seized at his shop was a treatise on pharmacy, with a card of the Blessed Virgin marking the place where the effects produced by the administration of copper sulphate were described. Another interesting piece of information which emerged from the enquiries was that his marriage contract had given him half the dowry only, so the death of his wife was necessary to ensure that he got the lot. It seems that his idea was to contract a third marriage which, with the proceeds of the second, would enable him to achieve his ambition to found a model pharmacy.

He had got away with the first murder without any suspicion of foul play. But with the second he was in too much of a hurry. At his trial, which took place in the same year as that of Boudas, he presented a striking contrast to the wild beast who was to share his execution day with him. He appeared in the dock, well-dressed and smiling, as if he were at some social gathering. His manner was easy-going and polite and he was obviously out to please. Reproached by the President of the court for having had, between his two marriages, relations with a married woman whose husband's state of health necessitated long absences at spas, and then for having taken over as his second wife the discarded mistress of a man who was prepared

to give a considerable dowry to get rid of her, Moreau replied
that all that mattered to him was that she should have come of
good family. But the President pointed out that what mattered
to the prosecution was the fact that he stood to make quite a
large profit, despite its scandalous origin. Moreau did not reply.
Judges in Britain listen to evidence and sum up dispassionately
for the benefit of the jury. In France, as we have seen in other
cases, the judge addresses the prisoner and throws the whole
book at him. The President went over the whole story in detail
from Moreau's days in the seminary; through his employment
with various pharmacists who found him to be a crooked and
underhand character; his military career; his first marriage
against the wishes of the bride's parents; the intermediate love
affair; the second marriage with the disgraceful dowry; up to
the exhumations. He quoted the exact quantities (confirmed by
expert analysts) of poison found in the remains. All that
Moreau could reply was that experts can make mistakes. 'You
should know, Moreau. You've studied pharmacy yourself!' said
the judge meaningly.

The mother of the second wife gave evidence and said that
when she noticed, after her daughter's death, that the body was
covered with black marks, Moreau answered coldly and
without shedding a tear, 'Well, decomposition had already
begun!'

When the last witness had been heard, Moreau was still
smiling cynically. The President remarked that he had little to
smile about which was true, for the next thing he heard was the
death sentence.

It was 14th October 1874, and, for the citizens of Paris, a
double event. That day had been chosen for the public execution by guillotine of the murderer Boudas and the poisoner

Moreau. The wolf-like killer with the receding forehead who had cut the unfortunate Faath almost to pieces in a blind fury, and the polite and gentlemanly Moreau with his scholar's brow, who had abandoned a vocation for the priesthood to murder two women slowly and in cold blood; in appearance and background they had nothing in common. Yet they were both killers for money, they both claimed to be innocent and they were finally united on a common execution date.

Twenty thousand people had been gathering outside La Roquette since one o'clock in the morning. At half past three, half a squadron of the *Garde Républicaine* had to be sent to clear the square and keep order. In the prison of La Roquette, both prisoners requested the ministrations of the Abbé Crozes, always on hand with Monsieur Claude when the guillotine was operating. Each prisoner had attended Mass on different days; although La Roquette had three death cells, there was only place for one condemned man in the prison chapel.

At four thirty, Claude went in turn into each of the cells with the Abbé Crozes and other officials to inform the prisoners that their pleas had been rejected and that the last hour had come. Moreau had slept well. As he dressed, he said, 'I am innocent!' The preliminaries must have been exaggerated since the execution was not to take place till six o'clock. In the meantime, Boudas was being prepared in another corridor of the prison.

It was Moreau's turn first. His *toilette* completed, he walked firmly to the guillotine outside the prison gate. A few steps away, he shouted out in a loud voice, 'All of you know! I die innocent.' He was pushed onto the plank and his head fell.

The blade went up again and was back in place in time for the appearance of Boudas. He did not know that the knife was already blooded. Less dignified than Moreau, he cried out that justice was committing a crime in killing him. 'Before God and all men, I am innocent!' were his last words. A few seconds later his head fell too. Claude reports that, as each head dropped into the basket, an 'ah!' of satisfaction went up from the whole crowd.

CHAPTER TWENTY-TWO

MONSIEUR CLAUDE IN LONDON

In 1869 a murder committed on a train between Calais and Boulogne involving two Englishmen – the killer and the killed – obliged Monsieur Claude to pay a visit to London, where he was entertained by his colleagues at Scotland Yard and taken on a tour of the Black Museum. Apart from his official business in London, however, his adventures on our side of the Channel can only be described as farcical.

It is quite incredible that the dreaded Monsieur Claude, *Chef de la Police de Sûreté,* the successor of Joseph Fouché, the confidant of cabinet ministers, the tactful manipulator in the high society scandals of the Second Empire and the terror of the underworld of Paris, could have behaved with such naïvety and allowed himself to become involved in one embarrassing situation after another. The British are reputed to be insular but at least they do live on an island and islanders are by nature insular. The French have no such excuse, yet are in many respects even more insular. The British are supposed to be bad linguists; even so, they did at one time colonize a large part of the earth and widely used sign language and pidgin English. The French, on the other hand, are among the worst linguists in the world. They have a delightful language which has been used internationally for centuries as the vehicle for diplomacy and good manners, so they do not bother to learn foreign languages in the way the Dutch, the Swedes or the Germans do. So we find Monsieur Claude launching himself in mid-Victorian England without knowing a word of English beyond the strange expression 'Pely-Coat-Bane', which is his version of Petticoat Lane. Still, I have known English tycoons who have gone to France as slenderly equipped linguistically as Monsieur Claude and with the same disastrous results.

Disaster overtook Monsieur Claude as soon as he landed at

Dover. The object of his visit to London was to take to Scotland Yard some papers stolen by a man called Williams, at that time awaiting extradition from Paris to London. Williams had murdered another Englishman on the Boulogne train. On arrival in Britain, Claude found that he had left his passport in his trunk which was travelling separately. The only papers he had on him were the papers stolen by Williams. Meanwhile the French police had advised Scotland Yard that Williams would be coming to London and that they were also sending the papers proving Williams to be the murderer. As far as the policeman at Dover was concerned, here was a man with incriminating papers and without a passport! The policeman drew his own conclusions, called up seven detectives and the Chief of the French police found himself under arrest. Speaking no English, Claude was quite helpless. They took no notice of his violent protestations and were unable to understand his explanation that his passport was in his trunk. When at last he managed to convey to them that he wanted to be taken to Scotland Yard, they told him in bad French that that was precisely what they were going to do with him, but that he would go by way of Newgate Prison. He was taken under guard to London and it was not until he was confronted at Scotland Yard with a solicitor whom he had known in Paris and who recognised him that poor Claude was freed. Excuses and apologies all round, but it was not an auspicious beginning.

He concluded his business and was taken on a tour of the Black Museum and the storehouse of stolen property which apparently formed part of it in those days. He was greatly impressed by our system of criminal records. In fact under the administration of Monsieur Claude's successor, reforms in the

Paris organisation, based on Claude's observations at Scotland Yard were instituted. After contemplating with appropriate philosophical remarks the various exhibits of the Black Museum; the stranglers' ropes, the cut-throat razors and the iron bars for smashing skulls, he was horrified at what he called the ferocity of London bandits. Little did he realise that his next adventure in London might well have added a further exhibit to the museum's collection.

After a day's discussions at the Yard, Monsieur Claude thought he would take a little time off to see things for himself before returning to France. I suppose most foreigners would set off to see the usual sights of London; not so Monsieur Claude! He could not have bought himself a map, since he had no idea where he was going. The superintendent who had been looking after him warned him of the dangers of going off the beaten track and the risk of attack by what Monsieur Claude described as 'buglars'. But Claude knew better. Without the slightest idea of where he was going, he followed the Thames, eastwards, and eventually found himself in Jack the Ripper territory east of Aldgate Pump, hardly the safest part of London a century ago. Jack the Ripper did not operate in that area until nearly twenty years later, but it was certainly not the place to be lost in at that time, and Claude was lost. He approached a sinister-looking character to ask the way home and was answered in good French. Claude was so surprised that he allowed the man to beg 'six pences' of him and to take him to a pub called the Eagle to drink a couple of pints and to be introduced into a company of anti-Bonapartist exiles. 'There you will find,' said the man, 'how we deal with Royalists and what we think of Hortense's bastard (Napoleon III)!' Indeed at the Eagle he found himself in a nest of anarchists and would-be regicides which filled him with a horror, far greater than he had experienced in the Black Museum. It was no place for the Chief of Police of Napoleon III and Claude decided it was time to move on. Just as he was going, he realised that he had been robbed. They were pick-pockets as well as anarchists. When he turned to ask his guide how this could have happened, the guide had disappeared. Claude left the pub and eventually found a policeman, who showed him the way home. Still, he did admit that he had been warned.

What fascinated Monsieur Claude most in our judicial system were the rituals and formalities connected with our method of execution by hanging. Having been present at a large number of executions by the guillotine – for Claude always followed his villains to the very end – he had to have a look at Newgate Prison, then on the site of the present Old Bailey and due to be demolished soon after Claude's visit.

He explained in his memoirs that executions were no longer public, as in France, and that the executioner received a fee equal to two hundred and fifty francs as well as being lodged and fed overnight in the prison. What hotel-keeper, asked Claude, would be willing to lodge the hangman for the night?

Unlike the executioner in France, whose only job is to see that the guillotine is in working order, the English hangman has to judge the weight and general build of his 'subject' in order to assess the drop. His sole concern is to ensure a quick death for the condemned man. Claude then gave a dissertation on strangulation as opposed to dislocation and explained how the knot was adjusted behind the left ear. Claude was impressed with the ritual of the solemn procession to the scaffold, the hoisting of a black flag over the prison as the hangman placed a yellow bag over the prisoner's head and released the trapdoor

211

spring. The hangman took leave of the governor of the prison after the black coffin had been brought and the proceedings concluded. What surprised Claude most was that the hangman's job was only a part time one; that he had to live in the country because living in London was so expensive; and had to have a regular job besides because he could not live on the fees which he was paid as a hangman.

Monsieur Claude eventually returned to Paris and many more triumphs in his own field. Since we have made fun of the worthy Monsieur Claude, let us leave the last word to him in his comment on the British: 'What a queer lot they are, our neighbours on the other side of the Channel!'

CHAPTER TWENTY-THREE

POST MORTEM

BEFORE COMMITTING MURDER IT IS ADVISABLE TO GIVE A LITTLE STUDY TO the interesting subject of forensic medicine. Forensic medicine or medical jurisprudence, to give it another imposing title, is the gentle art of making dead men tell tales. It is the science of applying all branches of medical knowledge to the purposes of the law. Now the law is there to protect us from harm, but if the law fails to act as a deterrent to those who successfully encompass our destruction, forensic medicine will go a long way towards bringing such individuals finally to book.

Let us suppose your body is discovered in circumstances which lead the police to think that 'foul play is suspected'. Unless there are half a dozen witnesses to testify that they saw the suspect drive a knife into you up to the hilt or administer to you four-and-a-half grains of arsenic or hold your head under the water in a bath for five minutes, your mortal remains will become a most interesting study in forensic medicine.

The range of knowledge required to discover why and how you came to your untimely death is a formidable one. First, Anatomy is needed to identify various parts of you should you have been dismembered, or to tell whether your remains are human or animal. Then come Surgery, to study the causes and effects of violence on your person; Toxicology, to establish the presence of poisons in your various organs; Botany, to recognise noxious plants you may have had administered to you; Chemistry, should you have vitriol thrown over you with evil intent; Physiology, to estimate your growth and development up to the time of your demise; and Pathology, the final dissection of your mortal remains, to discover any disease which may have accelerated your passing. Midwifery, Physics, *Materia Medica,* Criminal Psychology and other morbid studies, a reasonable appreciation of the nuances of the law and an insight

214

into the habits of cross-examining counsel all contribute to the vast armoury of the men who explode the 'perfect' murder.

The doctor's task is to save life by therapy, medicine, or surgery. The medical jurist on the other hand is concerned with death and is there to help the minions of the law either to bring the guilty to judgment or to establish the innocence of the falsely accused. He must therefore be a man with a suspicious mind and an all-seeing eye. He must be able to state as exactly as possible when death took place; must note all marks of violence, from the gash made by an axe to the tiny prick of a hypodermic needle; the direction and severity of wounds; and must decide whether you committed suicide or were saved the trouble. He will analyse the earth around you if you have been buried, as well as the contents of your stomach and intestines. He will inspect the powder marks, if any, and the path of the bullet through your body. He will examine pieces of the lungs in cases of suspected drowning or suffocation. He must know the effect of heat on the body, of fire or hot liquids or electricity, as well as the vagaries of lightning when it strikes a human body.

The contents of different organs, vomited matter, blood and other stains must all come under the microscope and be subjected to chemical tests. The brain and the spinal cord must be examined for injury and unusual conditions. Above all, the medical jurist must finally decide and be certain of the cause of death. The murderer therefore has a lot to reckon with, especially as the human body is a particularly difficult thing to destroy completely.

We have seen one classic masterpiece of forensic medicine in the case of Dr Ruxton. Another was the identification of the alkaloid, hyoscine, in the Crippen murder. We have even had a murder by insulin, the first of its kind, which could have remained undetected were it not for the experts of the Harrogate police laboratory and a number of other scientists and doctors, who worked together to break entirely new ground in establishing the cause of the death of a woman who had been found in a bath, apparently drowned in a faint.

In this modern age of technology, all manner of new poisonous substances are being used in products which can be obtained in any supermarket. The enormous number of medicinal drugs on the market grows every day. Each will call for new methods of detection if misused. We use increasingly large quantities of weed-killers and pesticides, which can kill us as efficiently as they destroy the stinging nettles on the garden path and the flies on the rose bushes.

Since Marsh discovered his test for arsenic well over a century ago, scientists have kept pace with killers and research goes on. Many of us, when studying the mistakes murderers have made in the past, have probably day-dreamed the perfect murder, but remember that they too thought they would never be found out!